DHARMA OCEAN SERIES

In a meeting with Samuel Bercholz, the president of Shambhala Publications, Ven. Chögyam Trungpa expressed his interest in publishing a series of 108 volumes, to be called the Dharma Ocean Series. "Dharma Ocean" is the translation of Chögyam Trungpa's Tibetan teaching name, Chökyi Gyatso. The Dharma Ocean Series consists primarily of edited transcripts of lectures and seminars given by Chögyam Trungpa during his seventeen years of teaching in North America. The goal of the series is to allow readers to encounter this rich array of teachings simply and directly rather than in an overly systematized or condensed form. At its completion, it will serve as the literary archive of the major works of this renowned Tibetan Buddhist teacher.

Series Editor: Judith L. Lief

DHARMA OCEAN SERIES

Orderly Chaos

THE MANDALA PRINCIPLE

Chögyam Trungpa

Edited by Sherab Chödzin

Shambhala · Boston & London · 1991

SHAMBHALA PUBLICATIONS, INC.
Horticultural Hall
300 Massachusetts Avenue
Boston, Massachusetts 02115

9 8 7 6 5 4 3 2

Printed in the United States of America on acid-free paper ⊗

Distributed in the United States by Random House, Inc., and
in Canada by Random House of Canada Ltd

Library of Congress Cataloging-in-Publication Data

Trungpa, Chogyam, 1939–
Orderly chaos : the mandala principle / Chögyam Trungpa.
        p.   cm.—(Dharma Ocean Series)
Includes index.
ISBN 0-87773-636-7 (alk. paper)
    1. Mandala (Buddhism) I. Title. II. Series.
BQ5125.M3T78   1991   91-52527
        294.3′438—dc20   CIP

Frontispiece photo by George Holmes, from the Vajradhatu Archives.

Contents

Editor's Foreword

The teaching of the Vidyadhara Chögyam Trungpa Rinpoche is that of the Kagyü and Nyingma lineages of Buddhism in Tibet, which is comprised of three major yanas, or vehicles: hinayana, mahayana, and vajrayana, or tantra. The culmination of the view, practice, and action of this teaching lies in the vajrayana. Therefore, in the vajrayana lies its greatest power and ultimate expression.

In these two seminars the Vidyadhara presents fundamental aspects of the vajrayana principle of mandala. Though speaking to an audience composed largely of beginners and near-beginners, he was bent on uttering the victory cry of the ultimate view. He wanted to give students who were or might be joining him an impression of the full depth and vastness of the teaching of his lineage. Conveying this to beginners meant bypassing the sophisticated apparatus of traditional Buddhist terms usually employed in describing this material. It meant condensing many layers of meaning into simple images, developing a sense of mandala on the spot using the language of everyday life in the West.

In introducing the mandala principle, the Vidyadhara asks the student to relate to a sense of totality that transcends "this and that." "This and that" is an ordinary expression employed by the Vidyadhara in a profound sense. You might ask someone what they talked about in a conversation and get the reply "this and that" or "one thing and another." To highlight the qualities of any "this," you have to contrast it with some "that." Contrasting "this" with "that" is the essence of ego's illusory game of duality, which it deliberately uses to obscure the total vision connected with the mandala principle.

Most fundamentally, "this" as opposed to "that" is ego, or self, as opposed to "other." "Other" can be whatever self is defining itself against at a given moment. Often people call that "the world" or "out there." Sometimes when talking about "this and that," in saying "this," the Vidyadhara would put his hand on his chest to betoken the sense of self.

There are infinite variations to the this-and-that game. Ego continuously uses these to maintain itself. Sometimes "this" is projected as overstuffed and hopeless and "that" as a roomy saving grace (as in, "Let's get out of here!"). The primary example is regarding all of "this" as samsara and opposing it to nirvana, the salvational "that" or somewhere-else. In fear or anger one is so trapped in the solidity of "this" that all of "that" becomes a threat. In fear one seeks to avoid "that," in anger to destroy it. From the ultimate point of view of ego, it does not matter how projections of this and that are shaped, weighted, and colored. All that matters is that the illusion of this and that is maintained any way at all. In this cynical *Realpolitik*, which is ego's ultimate insight, it comes ironically close to the total vision of mandala.

It was the Vidyadhara's incomparable genius to convey the most recondite teachings in everyday terms on the spot. The two seminars presented here are excellent examples. A reader looking for conventional conceptual sequences may at times be disappointed. He will, however, find ample consolation in an inexhaustible treasure-stream of experiential bull's eyes.

In editing this difficult material from the recorded tapes, I have had the good fortune to be able to consult a version prepared in 1976 by members of the New York City group of the Vidyadhara's students. I have found this helpful and would like to express my gratitude to those early editors.

SHERAB CHÖDZIN
NOVA SCOTIA 1990

ONE

Mandala
of Unconditioned Energy

KARME-CHÖLING 1972

I

Orderly Chaos

It seems there has been a lot of misunderstanding in the way the basic principle of mandala has been presented to people. Therefore, it is worth working further on the idea of mandala—what is mandala, why is mandala, how is mandala. This involves working with our life situation, our basic existence, our whole being.

To begin with, we should discuss the idea of orderly chaos, which is the mandala principle. It is orderly, because it comes in a pattern; it is chaos, because it is confusing to work with that order.

The mandala principle includes the mandala of samsara and the mandala of nirvana, which are equal and reciprocal. If we do not understand the samsaric aspect of mandala, there is no nirvanic aspect of mandala at all.[1]

The idea of orderly chaos is that we are confused methodically. In other words, the confusion is intentional. It is intentional in that we deliberately decide to ignore ourselves. We decide to boycott wisdom and enlightenment. We want to get on with our trips, with our passion, aggression, and so forth. Because of that, we create a mandala, a self-existing circle. We create ignorance deliberately, then we create perception, consciousness, name and form, sense-consciousness, touch, feeling, desire, copulation, the world of existence, birth, old age, and death.[2] That is how we create mandala in our daily existence as it is.

I would like to present the mandala principle from this everyday angle so that it becomes something workable rather than something purely philosophical or psychological, a Buddhist version of theology. From this point of view, orderly chaos is orderly, because we create the groundwork of this mandala. We relate to it as the ground on which we can play our game of hypocrisy and bewilderment. This game is usually known as ignorance, which is threefold: ignorance of itself, ignorance born within, and the ignorance of compulsion, or ignorance of immediate measure. (In the third ignorance, having developed a sense of separation from the ground, there is a feeling that we immediately have to do something about it.)

Since mandala is based on our ignorance and confusion, there is no point in discussing it unless we know who we are and what we are. That is the basis for discussing mandala. There is no point in discussing divinities, talking about which ones are located in which part of mandala diagrams, and about the principles that might quite possibly awaken us from our confusion into the awakened state.[3] It would be ludicrous to discuss those things at this point—completely out of the question. We have to know first what mandala is, why mandala is, and why such a notion as the notion of enlightenment exists at all.

The idea of enlightenment is born out of confusion. Because somebody is confused, there is the other aspect that contrasts with that confusion, which is enlightenment. We have to approach this scientifically: if confusion exists, then enlightenment exists, therefore confusion exists. We have to work with this polarity.

There is a sense of space, constantly. There is a sense of
space, because there is a boundary measuring the space. In
other words, if we had some land and we wanted to make a
definite statement that it was our land, we would have to put
up a fence around it. The fence would mean that this particular
area belonged to us and that we wanted to work on that basis.
With this approach, we get onto our land, we relate with it,
and we begin to possess it. It belongs to us. Then we develop
that sense of possession to the point where it is absolutely
impossible to work any further in that way. That space of our
land becomes solid space: It is *our* land, it completely belongs
to *us*. The whole land is *ours*. This sense of *ours* automatically
brings possessiveness, clinging to something, holding onto it.
Holding onto it means solidifying that land that belongs to
us. We concretize it as ours, we make it into concrete land,
concrete space. We freeze the whole area.

Consequently, the only thing left to relate with is the
boundary, the fence. That is the last hope we have. We begin
to look into that as a way of relating further. Maybe the fence
we set up originally might have some space in it. We begin
trying to eat up that fence like a worm, seeking territory or
spaciousness. Since we have no relationship with our basic
space as openness at all, we make the boundary into space.
This turns the whole thing upside down, like turning positive
film into a negative. Everything black turns white, and
everything white turns black. The only way left for us to relate
further is based on the hope that the fence might be a spacious
one—it might be hollow, not a solid wall. That is how we set
up a mandala situation to begin with, with our confused
mind.

Unfortunately, there is no point at all in relating with
everything as beautiful and glorious, as in a love-and-light
trip. That would be totally ludicrous, if I may say so.
Impractical. If we are going to freeze the whole area that we

have, then we have to relate with some other areas that might be space from that point of view. The proper introduction to mandala is to find out whether we are regarding the mandala as space or whether we are freezing that space and treating the situation around it as open space.

The whole thing could become quite workable. In other words, if nirvana exists, samsara exists equally. Are we going to relate with both together, or are we going to consider nirvana alone as workable and samsara as something we have to reject and destroy? This last kind of simpleminded approach is very confusing and, in fact, self-destructive. And that seems to be the point of relating with the mandala principle in terms of whether we have ground to discuss it at all or not. What is the ground? Is the ground solid space, or is the ground space-space?

STUDENT: I don't understand what a mandala basically is.

TRUNGPA RINPOCHE: It is space to create a situation that is based on a territory or boundary. It depends on whether we relate with space as space or space as solid, or with boundary as space or the other way around. That's how it goes.

STUDENT: When you speak about the boundary of the mandala, it sounds like you are talking about the boundary of us or the mandala of us. When we go to explore the boundary of the mandala, is that something like exploring our limits?

TRUNGPA RINPOCHE: That depends on our attitude toward the space, how we see it.

S: I see it as pretty solid.

TR: Then the boundary becomes the space, which brings a tremendous struggle.

S: That comes from separating space and solidity?

TR: It's something like the lost-wax method used by crafts-men. We expect the wax will act as the expression rather than what is inside it. It is exactly the same here. Experience becomes very claustrophobic. Naturally. And then it depends on whether we accept the claustrophobia as it is or not.

S: It becomes claustrophobic in that we are surrounded by a boundary?

TR: Yes.

S: What is it as it is?

TR: Your guess is as good as mine.

S: Are you describing an energy pattern of some kind?

TR: Well, obviously, yes. There is energy involved in dealing with the texture of things as they are. But the question is, are we willing to relate with the space, or are we involved with the boundary? Or are we willing to give up the whole trip of boundary and space and provide the basic ground?

S: Isn't the space the same as the basic ground?

TR: It depends on how you look at it.

STUDENT: Why is the mandala necessary? Can't we get along just as well without it?

TRUNGPA RINPOCHE: Sure, we don't have to have a man-dala at all, that's true. It is unnecessary. But that in itself becomes a mandala.

S: What does?

TR: The unnecessariness of it becomes a mandala. I mean, it's not a conceptual principle, it's what is. We don't have to call it a mandala or anything else. But it happens there.

S: Is it an organizational energy?

TR: Sure. Anyway, there is some unity there and some

pattern in it. The mandala is not important, but the mandala *happens*.

S: Are you saying that when we are relating to space as concrete and trying to eat out from inside the boundary, then we are not seeing the mandala aspect of things; but when we relate to the open, spacious aspect of it, then we begin to relate to it as a mandala?

TR: It's up to you, purely up to you. There's no philosophical definition of it at all. What we are doing here is not trying to get together set patterns and ideas, ideologies or theologies. We are not trying to develop a set idea of what a mandala is or isn't. We are more trying to relate to what a mandala might be or could be. There is no dogma involved at this point at all. It is more a question of developing a working basis for working together.

S: Is it a way of looking at the world?

TR: I suppose you could say that, yes. But it would be more accurate to say it's a way of seeing it.

S: Is there both a collective mandala and individual mandalas? So that each of us—

TR: Definitely, yes. That's how we perceive the world.

S: Then our own personal mandala is subject to change as we change our consciousness and our way of seeing it.

TR: We don't *change* our consciousness. It's subject to how our consciousness *grows*.

STUDENT: Could we work on creating a mandala for this seminar group?

TRUNGPA RINPOCHE: Sure, but you can't pin down the mandala principle as being this or that. We are discussing a totality in a blade of grass. Where there is grass growing, is that solid grass, or is it hollow grass in the midst of concrete space? Do you see what I mean? Can anyone explain?

S: It's like the figure-and-ground relationship. Is the grass the figure and . . . ?

TR: Yes. Do we describe the grass as outstanding in the midst of space, or do we say that the grass is the space and around the grass is the solidity? Do you see what I mean?

STUDENT: Is it more accurate to describe what is by saying a blade of grass is a hollow thing with solidity all around it? Is that more accurate?

TRUNGPA RINPOCHE: I think that is more accurate, yes.

STUDENT: Is it like the difference between simply considering a single thing and considering the total situation of the thing?

TRUNGPA RINPOCHE: Both amount to the same thing, because they are interdependent. You can't have just one or the other.

STUDENT: I don't understand what you mean by "giving up the trip of space and providing the basic ground."

TRUNGPA RINPOCHE: That's giving up the whole thing with the interdependent elements—whether grass is the space or whether grass is the object.

S: Giving all that up?

TR: Giving up that *whole* area. Then there is the possibility of some complete working basis. The tantric tradition on the kriya yoga level talks about preparing the mandala with the five ingredients of a cow.[4] The five ingredients are the snot of a cow, shit of a cow, piss of a cow, milk of a cow, and so forth. Clean up the holy ground with those, going beyond discrimination. Clean the ground completely with the five ingredients of a cow, then you can build a mandala on it, or make a sand painting, or just lines. From the tantric point of view, that is the only workable situation—you have destroyed or overcome the hollow space or solid space in order to create the true mandala, the absolute mandala. This is not purely superstition, you know, this kriya yoga idea of the five ingredients of a cow. The cow belongs to the earth. It grazes and sits and shits and eats grass and lives on the land. It has the quality of a sitting bull. And the five ingredients come out of that cow or sitting bull. It's a tremendously powerful thing to smear it over the whole phenomenal world, the snot and milk and piss and shit and everything. It's fantastic! It evens out the whole thing. It's beautiful!

STUDENT: Is the ground the middle path?

TRUNGPA RINPOCHE: No, I wouldn't even say it is the middle path. There's nothing middle about it. It's *the* ground that does not allow any compromise. It's not in the middle— it's *the* ground. It has nothing to do with the middle at all.

S: Could it be just not dwelling on anything?

TR: I suppose you could say that, but let me explain about mandala principle as a whole. It is part of the tantric situation, the tantric approach. We are not discussing madhyamaka or the shunyata principle.[5] We are discussing the basic existence of things as they are—how we survive, how we live. So the whole thing becomes less philosophical. There's no middle path involved. There's a total path. This is an absolutely heavyhanded approach to things as they are. There's no middle way at all. It's heavy-handed.

STUDENT: It seems that we haven't even approached the madhyamaka level properly. How can we work with what you are talking about now without distorting it?

TRUNGPA RINPOCHE: We can do so theoretically, but

from the point of view of actual practice, we should sit and meditate and work on ourselves in a basic fashion. What we are discussing is the possible chaos that might happen, the orderly chaos that might happen as we go along the path. This seminar could be regarded as a warning session. Somebody who hasn't yet learned how to drive can still study the highway codes and how to relate with motor cars. It is possible that chaos, orderly chaos, might happen in our situation. In that regard, I personally feel that I can trust the American audience comprised of those who are on the path or might be on the path. I feel brave enough to tell them what the path is all about. I feel that I can relate with them and explain all the possibilities of order and chaos. I feel telling them about it might create some awakeness on the path. It's a situation of preparing the whole ground rather than purely a matter of immediate instruction. You have to commit yourself to the path and surrender yourself to it. You have to take refuge, become a refugee, to begin with—give up everything. Then you have to be willing to take the responsibility of a bodhi-sattva.[6] Then after that, you can receive the tantric teachings. But that seems to be a long way off as far as we are concerned. Nevertheless, it is worth discussing the possibility of these situations occurring for all of us.

STUDENT: Does the basic ground come about when you somehow forget about the "this" and the "that," the discrimination? Is that what you are implying?

TRUNGPA RINPOCHE: Yes.

S: And this is experiential, not just intellectual.

TR: Yes.

S: How do you know when you have experienced it?

TR: It's purely up to you.

S: It seems to me there could be some self-deception.

TR: If you are experiencing things completely and totally, that means that you have worn out your reference point. That is a total experience.

S: Worn out your reference point?

TR: As though you are completely dead, or at least dying. You have no way of referring to anything alive, you are actually dying. It's very solid and very simple.

STUDENT: It seems to me that the most difficult thing to do is to get over a sense of separation. Isn't that what this is about? Interdependence depends on separation, and if you could give that up, then you could relate to a totality. But how does one do that?

TRUNGPA RINPOCHE: You don't have to know how to do it. It just happens. There is no special care or "idiot compassion" from the teacher or the teaching. You simply have to work it out. You have to acknowledge that you are a lonely person, a person alone, treading on the path.

S: But doesn't the sense of aloneness or loneliness contradict the idea of totality?

TR: Absolutely not. If you realize that you are a lonely person, then you feel the totality of the whole space in which you are lonely or alone. It amounts to the same thing, absolutely the same thing. You can't feel alone unless you feel the totality of the whole thing. There is no help coming from anywhere at all. You have to make your own individual journey, which is purely based on you. That goes without saying.

S: That's not the same thing as ordinary loneliness then.

TR: There is no such thing as ordinary loneliness. Loneliness is one thing—there is always space.

We are going to introduce discussion groups tomorrow, which could be extraordinarily important at this point. They will provide an opportunity for people to relate with each other and to express their chaos and confusion in terms of the mandala principle. They will be able to open themselves and discuss their ideas.

The situation we have is that our philosophers and yogis are at war. The yogis think the philosophers are bullshitting, and the philosophers think the yogis are bullshitting. As a result, at this point we are unable to establish a total living teaching, which would mean not rejecting either of those. So what we are trying to do is establish some link between the two, so that the approaches of both philosophers and yogis could both be regarded as valid. Some technical or intellectual understanding is important, and your experiential situation is also important. Working those two together is extraordinarily possible.

The expectation is that eventually I won't have to give any more seminars. You will be able to help youselves. Not only that, but you will be able to develop American Buddhism, to teach other people, to teach the rest of the world. In fact, you will be able to go back to the Tibetans or the Indians and teach them what their earlier understanding was all about and work with them.

As far as I personally am concerned, I have tremendous trust in your participation in this work, and it means a lot to me that finally we are able to work together on the basic sanity level, that we are able to set up some solid ground enabling you to help your whole world, not purely in terms of religion but also in terms of concrete living situations.

Participation in the discussion groups tomorrow will be an expression of acceptance that we are going to work together, as opposed to your simply being here to pick up something, some spark of knowledge, and take it back home and maybe write a fat book on it. The situation doesn't work that way. It very much needs sharing. So please take part in the discussion groups and also the meditation practice with our community here; that is also part of the seminar. It is very important to give in to the irritations and frustrations that take place in meditation practice. Thank you very much and welcome everybody.

The Razor's Edge

The problem in discussing the idea of mandala seems to be that it is extraordinarily abstract. We see it as a metaphysical or philosophical principle, so we cannot learn anything about it unless some emphasis is made on a pragmatic way of looking at the idea of mandala. We have to have some working base or some way of identifying ourselves with the basic mandala principle. We have to see how the mandala principle is connected with a learning process or a practicing process. As has been said already, the only way to do that is to relate with the basic ground in which the mandala exists.

The word *mandala* literally means "association," "society." The Tibetan word for mandala is *kyilkhor. Kyil* means "center," *khor* means "fringe," "gestalt," "area around." It is a way of looking at situations in terms of relativity: if that exists, this exists; if this exists, that exists. Things exist interdependently, and that interdependent existence of things happens in the fashion of orderly chaos.

We have all kinds of orderly chaos. We have domestic orderly chaos and we have the emotional orderly chaos of a love affair. We have spiritual orderly chaos, and even the attainment of enlightenment has an orderly chaos of its own.

So it is a question of relating with different types of orderly chaos.

But before discussing the idea of orderly chaos itself, we have to discuss the basic area in which orderly chaos happens. Before we realize something is orderly and before we realize that it is chaos, there is some basic ground on which that chaos is constantly happening in an orderly fashion, in accordance with its own pattern. This ground is what we are concerned with now in our discussion of mandala. Seeing the ground is connected with how we can wake ourselves up, how we practice, how we relate with the day-to-day situation.

I would like to repeat and make very clear that we cannot discuss the higher mandala principle until we have some realization concerning the samsaric or confused mandala, the confused level of orderly chaos. The basic situation is that we are involved in a sense of struggle in our lives. We are trying to defeat somebody or win somebody over, to get rid of an enemy or acknowledge a friend. Whether we live in the city or in the country, we are trying either to fight with our environment or to indulge in it.

There are all kinds of areas where we are constantly involved with picking and choosing. That is the basic area where the orderly chaos is taking place. Spirituality, from a superficial point of view, is based on the idea of making things harmonious. But somehow, from the point of view of the mandala principle, that approach does not apply. The idea is not so much to make things harmonious and less active, but to relate with what is happening, with whatever struggles and upheavals are going on—trying to survive, to earn more dollars, get more food, more room, more space, a roof over our heads, and so on. If we are living in the city or certain areas in the suburbs, it could be extraordinarily oppressive. Possibilities of rape and murder are taken for granted, and things seem to happen of their own accord. We never know what is the beginning, what is the end, or how to proceed.

As soon as we wake up in the morning, we find that we are ready to fight the world. Having breakfast is a preparation, like taking a magic potion so that we can fight the world. And after having breakfast, we go out and fight the world. There is something interesting and very beautiful about the simplicity of preparing for warfare and then beginning to fight. We either expect to be attacked and defend ourselves or attack somebody else and have them defend themselves. So we are going to have an encounter that is based on struggle. No matter what our particular mentality is, the total picture is one of struggle—fight, gain, and loss. That kind of basic mentality exists whether we live in a town or in the country. That mentality goes on constantly. The sense of the total environment is one of abstract struggle.

It is not struggle for something particular or on behalf of a particular syndicate or anything like that; rather there is a total sense of imprisonment. There is a sense that the world has captured us and we have to live with it, we have to fight it as though we were behind iron bars. The sense of imprisonment is always there. That is the basic ground of the mandala, before orderly chaos begins to happen.

There is that total area of depression or excitement, of expressing richness or poverty; something is holding us to that particular place. That fundamental totality of grayness or black-and-whiteness—it depends on the individual—is interesting, extraordinarily beautiful, if I may use such a term. By beautiful, I do not mean something purely pleasurable; I am referring to the fact that the ground is extremely awake, alert. Everybody is alert, willing to fight, willing to attack, willing to make money, willing to struggle with the living situation in whatever way. There is that whole, total energy that we are involved with. There is constantly a sense that something is just about to take place. It is as though some underground gossip network had sent a message around, and everybody has decided to be prepared for the situation. The five-minute warning has already been given, all over the place. There is a kind of tentative flickering of positive and negative possibilities—possible chaos, possible gift of God. We can look at it from either side—possible excitement, possible depression. There is that flickering going on in the background of the whole situation.

The reason I am mentioning this is because that situation is not solid space. It is actual space, and we could feel a sense of "spaceness" all the time. There is some element of free will always there. Even if we feel trapped or compelled to do certain things, nevertheless we feel that the decision and the spaciousness—this sense of space, this sense that something is taking place—belongs to us. Of course, this is a very abstract point, very difficult to grasp.

That total energy—totally creative, totally destructive—is what one might call nowness. Nowness is the sense that we are attuned to what is happening. The past is fiction and the future is a dream, and we are just living on the edge of a razor blade. It is extraordinarily sharp, extraordinarily tentative and quivering. We try to establish ground but the ground is not solid enough, because it is too sharp. We are quivering between that and this.

Living on the razor blade means at the same time living in the total space, because the possibility exists that it might cut us through, destroy us, and the possibility also exists that we might be able to avoid the razor's cut. But both those possibilities amount to the same thing at this point. The sense of the razor blade's sharpness is very interesting, extraordinarily interesting. That is what we call intelligence, primordial intelligence. We feel that razor blade's sharpness and its cutting quality. We sense that, we feel it, and we also want to run away from it. We would rather sit or perch on something more solid, like a toilet seat, some place where there's no razor blade. But when we are on the razor blade, such an invitation becomes a fantasy. That is our basic intelligence beginning to sense all kinds of areas that are impossible but still somehow possible at the same time. This happens all the time.

It could actually be said to be a gift of God that we have not been presented with a comfortable toilet seat to perch on. Instead we've been presented with a razor blade for a seat. You never perch on a razor blade, you just *be* on it with attentiveness. The razor blade is an expression of the space of all the other areas. It could be that the rest of the areas are threatening and the razor blade is a comfortable space to sit on, or that the other areas are inviting and the razor blade is threatening. Whatever the case may be, there is that sense of being there fully, with nothing tentative about it at all. The whole thing becomes extremely powerful and spacious, and that is the enlightened or transcendental aspect of the mandala.

The enlightened aspect of the mandala and the samsaric, or whirlpool-like, aspect take place on the same razor blade. But actually there is not just one razor blade. The path is full of razor blades, to such an extent that we have nowhere to walk. We might wish for the yogic ability to levitate so that we could avoid these razor blades, but we find that we have not acquired that ability yet. If we had, then quite possibly there would be no razor blades there at all. Being able to levitate and there not being any razor blades amount to the same thing.

This razor-blade quality is something more than psychological irritation. Life as a whole becomes penetratingly sharp—unavoidable and at the same time cutting. We could say that that is the living description of the truth that life contains pain. According to Buddhism, life or existence is defined according to the truth of suffering, which is the razor blade.

The truth of the origin of suffering is finding out that there *is* a razor blade. Then there is the truth of the goal, which is connected with seeing the razor blade as the path, or else diminishing the effect of the razor blade. But we cannot use magical powers at all. We have to face the reality in its fullest truthful nature, straightforwardly.

STUDENT: We are always thinking about the past or dreaming about the future, and it seems you are saying that as our awareness that we are caught up in this process grows, we begin to feel our pain more directly. And instead of trying to do away with it, we have to get into it. We have to just see that that's the way we are, more and more. Is that what you are saying?

TRUNGPA RINPOCHE: The point is not to philosophize. You can say that the effect of our awareness is thus-and-such, therefore if we accept or reject the pain, that's our bad luck. But we don't approach it from that angle. Pain contains a very interesting level of subtlety that we could relate with. To begin with, what do we really mean by pain? Are we talking about physical pain or psychological pain? Physical pain is connected with our attitude toward our body and our attitude toward our environment. In other words, pain contains a mystical experience (if we could use such an expression) within itself. If we relate to pain fully, there is tremendous depth in it. We begin to realize the cutting quality of the razor-edge of the pain, which severs beliefs in this and that. It cuts right through us. When we really and truly experience psychological pain as it is, we have no room at all to create conceptual ideas of this and that. We just experience pain fully and directly.

The point is not just accepting as a philosophy that we should be in a state of equilibrium and consider pain random and just sit on it. There is something more than that—there is an intelligent way of relating to pain. Pain is there because of you, and you try to struggle with the pain over who is going to win: Are you going to win or is the pain going to win? Those battles between you and the pain are unnecessary. If you become the pain completely, then without *you,* pain's function becomes nothing. It is just energy, just sharpness of something. It might still cut through, but it is no longer pain as we know it.

You see, the problem is that we do not experience pain as pain at all. We only experience the *challenge* of the pain, the challenge of whether or not we are going to overcome the pain.[That is why we feel pain—because we feel that we are going to lose our territory and the pain is going to take us over.] That is where the real pain begins on the ordinary level. So if we give up the struggle and become the pain completely, fully, then the pain is me and I am the pain. That is exactly what the Buddha meant when he spoke of duhkha as the *truth* of suffering. There is truth in suffering, which is self-existing truth rather than observed truth on a relative level.

STUDENT: Does that mean trusting that the truth of the pain will be transforming?

TRUNGPA RINPOCHE: Somewhat, yes. You could say that it transforms into a sharpness or energy and is no longer pain as a challenge.

STUDENT: Could you explain what the function of masochism or hypochondria is in this connection?

TRUNGPA RINPOCHE: Hypochondria or masochism are still related to the challenge of the battlefield. You still let yourself be challenged, which is not actually identifying with the pain. You're dealing with the fringe alone, and you don't experience the pain in its fullest sense at all.

S: What about asceticism?

TR: Asceticism takes an entirely different approach to pain. Here you have the idea that you are going to benefit from pain, rather than rejecting it, feeling bad about it. That is quite interesting. It is like mothers who enormously enjoy labor pain, because it means something to them. They are going to give birth. Or it is like experiencing or perching on the pain of diarrhoea; this experience of pain is worthwhile, because you're going to get rid of your diarrhoea, you're going to give birth to something, you're going to clean it completely out of your system and get rid of it. That is the approach to pain that we find in asceticism. It is worthwhile experiencing it: let's do it, let's get through it. But there is something very suspicious about that as well. It is very suspicious when asceticism exists purely for its own sake.

There could also be asceticism as a way of openness and experiencing pain fully. But asceticism is actually transcended at that point. At that point, you just become a simple person, an *anagarika,* which means "homeless one." You can be a true homeless one, or you can also be a false homeless one, because you are still looking for some feedback about having given up your home. That way your homelessness provides a home for you to be in. That is a very subtle point. So true homelessness is just giving up without taking on anything new; it is just simplifying yourself without questioning what you are going to get in return.

STUDENT: It sounds as if it would be very easy to fall into an approach to pain of congratulating yourself on how much of it you're feeling and seeing.

TRUNGPA RINPOCHE: Well, yes, that's the whole point. You can regard the pain as pain or you can regard it as part of your projection, which is an entirely different area. If you regard pain as something coming from outside, challenging you from the outside, but still you give in to it, that is suicidal. But if you regard pain as something that is there, that is part of your state of mind, and you take the approach of not feeding the pain anymore, that is another matter altogether.

STUDENT: Since you're saying that pain is there all the time, would that mean that when you're not feeling the pain, the psychological pain, that you're more asleep—that in a sense seeking the painful aspect of a situation would be moving toward being more awake?

TRUNGPA RINPOCHE: Yes, I suppose so. But that is very, very dangerous to say.

S: What about the pain that has to do with the distance I feel between you and me?

TR: That's the same thing again, exactly. You are trying to live with your expectations of how that pain might not come about.

S: Or the pain between the people in the house here.

TR: Yes, it's the same thing. Something is not feeding you, something is not comforting you. You feel that the discomfort is about to take you over and you are trying to fight that, rather than actually being concerned about the distance between you and the object of communication, such as the distance between you and me. That seems to be out of view at the time you are feeling the problem. Your relationship with the pain becomes the problem at that point, because of the pretense of some logic that is hovering about in your state of mind, which really has nothing to do with it, in fact. From that point of view, the problem is that we feel our pain is a problem.

STUDENT: Are you making a distinction between an active

and a passive approach to pain? By active, I mean: I'm going to figure out a way of reacting to this pain so that I can become more aware; and passive would be just feeling it.

TRUNGPA RINPOCHE: I don't think there is any difference. It seems to be the same thing, because wherever pain, or duhkha, happens, it always has entirely the same nature, the same style, and the same type of approach. The idea is always: something's just about to take me over, now I have to resist that. And then there is logical mind: this is happening because somebody has ill-treated me or rejected me, or whatever. In fact, that logical mind is a facade. There is the sense that somebody might take me over and the challenge of how to regain my power in terms of my being and my consciousness, my emotions—that seems to be the crucial point. And the logic—such as, he killed my father, therefore I should try to kill him—is actually beside the point. It is just an excuse, in fact. It has nothing to do with the pain at all. The actual pain is that sense that something has to be overcome, to be conquered. In other words, the whole idea of pain is fighting yourself, fighting your concept with your intellect.

STUDENT: I feel that there is real suffering and misery in this world, and all of these things that we've been talking about sometimes feel to me like a thousand-dollar bill that I can't spend to do anything about it. It feels like these points of view don't enable me to do anything actual about pain and suffering in this world.

TRUNGPA RINPOCHE: I think you could do a lot. The reason why there is the chaos of struggling with pain in the world is that we haven't come to terms with what pain actually is ourselves, personally. If we can come to an understanding of pain in our own innate nature, we will then be dealing with the situation directly, and there will be less pain. The pain becomes purely chaos, orderly chaos.

The pain doesn't have to be there. If you want to stop the war in Vietnam, you have to stop *your* pain, your version of the Vietnam war. You have to relate with your own antagonism, your own innate war between you and your projections. If you solve that problem and relate with that transmutation process, then it will become much easier to solve the problem existing on the diplomatic or international level. That problem then becomes just purely a bundle of instances that occurred on the basis of orderly logic, the end result of which was chaos. It is the same orderly chaos that is happening all the time, and one can handle it beautifully at that point. The problem now is that we cannot keep track of the situation. We look at national or international things so much in terms of our own projections that we lose track of the actual political situation.

S: On the whole, if we can let go of the reference point of the self and relate with the pain directly, we will end up creating less pain.

TR: I think so, yes. But if you rely on that as a promise or reassurance, you end up destroying the whole thing.

3

The Portrait of Confused Mind

We have discussed the basic area of sitting on the razor blade, which is the area of passion, aggression, and ignorance. It is the basic area where the samsaric mandala can be established or constructed. We can now go into further details about the samsaric mandala itself.

Sitting on the razor blade in the manner of passion, aggression, and ignorance creates tremendous room for working with the next situation. The way we work with the next situation is not by trying to get rid of anything or to become a better person, but by finally acknowledging our actual situation.

What we discussed in the last talk was the area of the basic styles of all kinds that we evolve in relating with life situations so that we can accommodate mind's neurosis. We have all kinds of styles of perching, sitting on the razor's edge, and we also have developed the style of spiritual materialism, which is constantly trying to substitute one myth for another. Out of that level comes something else that goes beyond that level. There is a definite move in our confused mind, which happens in accordance with the basic character of the mandala: we decide to become deaf and dumb. We decide no longer to be sensitive to what our life situation is all about. In other words, the battlefield situation of fighting against something else is accepted without question. We feel that we have to get our money's worth out of the struggle. We feel we have to continue until we get our reward for that struggle or until we have a sense that the struggle has been fulfilled. We are not going to accept just anything, because we think we are too smart to go along with things out of blind faith. We think we have to get something out of our situation, gain something. If we are practicing meditation or involved with spirituality, we want to attain enlightenment. We feel that if we do not attain enlightenment, we will have been cheated. And up to the point where it becomes clear that we have been cheated, we are willing to remain deaf and dumb. If we hear that we can attain enlightenment through a meditation practice that con- sists of standing on our heads twenty-four hours a day, we will do it. We will reduce ourselves to a state of deaf and dumb until we reach the end result and get our money's worth. All the promises that are made to us target this kind of ignorance. We are blinded by the promises, by their glaring, flashing, colorful aspect. We let ourselves be blinded by the promises and go through the pain of being blinded by the promises. We are willing to let ourselves be reduced to a state of deaf and dumb.

That is the ignorance that constitutes the central part of the samsaric mandala. We are willing to give into everything as long as there are promises that are seemingly worth giving in to. Having heard some "word of wisdom" telling us that it is worthwhile to give in, we forget the experiential path. We walk the path like a blind man. We avoid being sensitive to whatever life situations we encounter on the way.

This ignorance forms the basic structure of the mandala that is the ground for both spiritual and psychological mate- rialism. Spiritual materialism develops because we are willing to take a chance on all kinds of trips, like holding a grain of sand in our hand and meditating on that for three months, or fasting for ten months. We fall for all kinds of promises. It is true, if you keep holding that grain of sand, when the time is up, obviously you will have accomplished that. It is a tremendous accomplishment—you will become an enlightened grain-of-sand holder. That is certainly an accomplishment, undoubtedly.

There is also an element of ordinary psychological materialism that develops as part of the mandala experience. This takes the form that, in order to work toward a goal, we are willing to ignore the nature of the path to it, the eccentricity of that path. For example, in order to become president of the country, you have to go through all kinds of eccentric trips. You have to make all kinds of promises and keep changing your mind back and forth in order to seduce the voters. Whatever you have to do to win, you go through the whole thing and make a fool out of yourself, because if you are willing to make a fool out of yourself, an absolutely perfect fool, then you get to become president. So there is that kind of bravery, being willing to insert yourself into those kinds of situations and getting involved in their speed. There are all kinds of examples of this. Needless to say, people are quite familiar with this whole approach.

The eccentricity trip that a candidate for president goes through involves believing in the deaf-and-dumb aspect of the journey. We ignore everything except what we come out as in the end when we become president. Whatever we have to go through in the process is acceptable. We reduce ourselves to a state of deaf and dumb. We become hardened, hardened travelers. That can be seen as making us even greater, and we tend to become heroes of some kind because of our hardened quality of being deaf and dumb.

This kind of approach provides the central part of the

samsaric mandala. Then there are the four quarters of the mandala.

Aggression is connected with the eastern quarter of the mandala. Aggression in this sense is based on intellect and analytic mind. You cannot become an aggressive person unless you know what to be aggressive about. Being aggressive automatically entails some kind of logic. Whether that logic is logical or illogical makes no difference. Your logic is founded on a platform that you can land on or crash on, which is basic aggression. Aggression involves an extremely severe attitude toward yourself. You are not willing to entertain yourself, enjoy yourself, treat yourself well at all. You constantly have a war going on between that and this, so in order to defeat whatever it may be, you have to be aggressive, pushy; you have to come down heavy and sharp all the time. Whether you are involved in spiritual or psychological materialism, the basic approach is the same. There is a kind of austerity.

We find that many of the aggressive people in history have been very austere. Aggressive people will not let themselves be entertained. They are willing to sacrifice their health and their comfort as part of being aggressive, pushy, penetrating, cutting, destructive. They would rather stick with that than let anyone touch them in a gentle and loving way. If you are such a person, and you get near any loving situation—for example, someone wants to stroke your head—you regard it as an insult: "Don't touch me, I'm on this logic trip. Don't try to mind my business." It is a very individualistic approach. There is no room for compromise, because logic is saying yes or no constantly, all the time.

The southern quarter of the samsaric mandala is connected with pride. It is actually more arrogance or a self-enriching quality than pride in the ordinary sense. Ordinarily, when you say you are a proud person, there is an element of confidence involved. But the pride we are talking about is without dignity or confidence; it is simply self-assertive. It is arrogant in the sense that you are not willing to let yourself be regarded as needing to be rescued or saved. Not only that—you want to be acknowledged. You want people to acknowledge your richness or your potentiality for richness so that you can march into other people's territory. If necessary, you are willing to roll into their territory, expand into it.

The image of this type of arrogance is a gigantic tank of honey being released. Waves and waves of sweet, gooey honey roll in your direction as you relate to an arrogant person of this type. There is no question about it, the honey is going to come. Slow and dignified in its own limited way, it is coming toward you. This is a perverted way of demonstrating richness. There's no room for questioning—this richness simply descends on you. The person might constantly give you rich gifts of food and money. You are presented with gifts until you have to run away from the horror of this generosity. It becomes outrageous, overwhelming, demonic. There is no element of basic intelligence; it is simply heavy-handed. There may be some element of sharing, because that person also needs some comforting, but the approach to that becomes very heavy-handed too. Any sense of comfort or entertainment becomes more than is needed. It becomes uninviting and claustrophobic.

In the western quarter of the mandala is passion, or grasping. This is a mentality of tremendous suction. In relating to a seducer who is manifesting this passion, you get sucked in constantly. Your existence becomes less meaningful, because the existence of the seducer becomes more powerful than yours. You begin to regard yourself as just an insignificant snowflake that automatically melts when you get near the source of this suction. You are completely seduced, reduced to nothing, sucked in. The seduction of this passion asks you to become part of the seducer's territory rather than a partner.

There is no element of dance at all. Everything is continuously sucked in. There is no room for love in the sense of free exchange. Love becomes overwhelming. You are reduced to a part of the other person's love rather than having the free choice of making love yourself. Your beauty and dignity and glamour become part of the other person's power of suction. You become just a grain of metal with this gigantic lump of a magnet drawing you in, and you have no hold on anything. There's no room for questioning. You are completely melted, sucked in.

In many cases, people want something like this to happen, because they actually do regard themselves as insignificant. They want to be loved, they want to be sucked in. But even people who have esteem for themselves as individual entities cannot help themselves once they are confronted with the extraordinarily powerful suction of the western quarter of the mandala.

Next is the northern quarter of the mandala, from which jealousy comes. It is not exactly jealousy; we do not seem to have the proper term in the English language. It is a paranoid attitude of comparison rather than purely jealousy, and this becomes a very heavy-handed factor as you find yourself invited to compare yourself with *that* all the time. This sense of comparison becomes heavy-handed because you see *that* situation as richer than this one. One finds one's own situation lacking and tries to bloat it up like a bloated corpse. There is a logical mentality of comparison. "Since that is bigger than me, I should build myself up until I am much bigger than that." I try to build myself up to the point of being gigantic, huge, so that my sheer size can undermine the competition. So it is more than jealousy; it is a sense of competition.

Again, the game here is one of drawing the other in, rather than undermining or completely absorbing it. You do not want to absorb the object of jealousy, but you want to let it sit there and finally be completely undermined so you can crush it down. The sense of the jealousy says: That thing was bigger than me when we began, but now I'm becoming half its size, now I am its full size, and now I'm slightly bigger, now I'm much bigger, huge. Now I'm huge and great and gigantic and that thing out there has become insignificant for me. Nothing is threatening for me anymore at all.

Those five factors—ignorance in the center, anger in the east, pride in the south, passion in the west, and jealousy in the north—form a complete portrait of our world. From that point of view, we are the ideal mandala. In our limited way, we have all the richness and all the colorful and intelligent aspects of existence. Without discussing the negative aspects of the mandala, there is no way of understanding its positive aspects. The point now is to understand the complete psychological portrait of confused mind.

STUDENT: Could you explain pride a bit more. I didn't understand it very well.

TRUNGPA RINPOCHE: It's a question of trying to extend your territory by disregarding the object you are relating with. In other words, you demonstrate your richness and create a claustrophobic situation for others.

S: What is the honey symbolic of?

TR: The potential for that kind of richness has a sweet and all-pervasive quality, and that sweetness is overwhelming, gooey. Honey is sweet and seductive, but we can only relate with it to a very limited extent. We don't expect to *bathe* in honey. We just expect to taste a spoonful, which is already a lot. But when we find waves and waves of it descending upon us, it becomes extremely suffocating.

S: So pride is extremely suffocating?

TR: Yes.

S: Do others relate with it?

TR: We are already one of those others, and we are dying in it. The proud person himself or herself is expressing his or her death. But we are talking about it from the point of view of the other person at this point. That is the only way we can talk about it. That goes for all five principles. We have to talk about them from the point of view of the other person, the one who is watching, the victim of those things, rather than from the point of view of being in it. It is worthless talking about that. There's no point in talking about how you feel about it from the inside. How you feel is like being sick in a hospital, having a terrible pain. The best way of explaining the pain is from the point of view of a witness of your pain rather than looking into how you would express it yourself. That goes for death as well.

STUDENT: Rinpoche, what is the relationship between the center, deaf and dumb, and the four quarters?

TRUNGPA RINPOCHE: All four quarters function and conduct their process by being deaf and dumb, by relating to their particular situation without being sensitive.

S: Is the assignment of particular directions to the various qualities arbitrary, or is there some meaning to that?

TR: There is a relationship between east and west, north and south. There are polarities of anger and passion, pride and jealousy. There are polarities and pulls of all kinds that happen according to that pattern. It is not just random.

STUDENT: I don't understand why the portrait is so negative. Why are we taking this negative approach?

TRUNGPA RINPOCHE: If you understand the deaf-and-dumb aspect, that is the key to the whole thing. When we discuss the various negative qualities, we do not particularly talk about how to overcome them, but about how to realize the heavy-handedness of each one. That brings some clue of how to relate with it. The alchemistic approach of base metal changing into gold comes later.

S: Does one find oneself more in one of the areas of the mandala than in the others?

TR: You have your own feeling of the mandala, which is related to one part, but it is still partly related to all the others. There is still the deaf-and-dumb quality always there. You are not willing to let yourself see what is happening as your game. That factor is always there. We could say that we have a certain potential. Because we are one of the four, we have certain characteristics. We are not transparent people, so we each have our own heavy-handedness, which is exactly what makes the path necessary. The path is for the use of heavy-handed people. Because of their particular heavy-handedness, they are on the path. So we should not regard that as something bad that we have to reject or destroy.

STUDENT: In our discussion group we were saying that no matter how heavy-handed we are, we do somehow perceive the game quality of our trip as we are doing it.

TRUNGPA RINPOCHE: Except that we decide to play deaf and dumb. Understanding is how we play the game in this case.

S: What's the alternative to playing deaf and dumb?

TR: Not playing it.

S: What do you do?

TR: You don't do anything.

S: You mean being spontaneous.

TR: Well, spontaneity has all kinds of derogatory connotations connected with being loose.

S: I was thinking of the positive aspect of being spontaneous.

TR: But even then, it can become quite trippy. When you talk about spontaneity, it seems to mean just doing what's there, letting loose, which is a rather primitive and simpleminded idea of freedom. It's not just a question of being spontaneous. You are spontaneous because there is a certain intelligence functioning with the spontaneity. We'll come to that when we talk about the anti-ignorance aspect of the five principles. The idea of spontaneity involves being generous at the same time. But you could be overwhelmed by your generosity and get sucked into it. Then you might become frivolous rather than spontaneous. It's extremely sensitive.

STUDENT: In that case, where does discipline fit in?

TRUNGPA RINPOCHE: Precisely there. You have to discipline your spontaneity with intelligence. That way spontaneity has an element of orderly chaos in it. In talking about orderly chaos, we could say that *orderly* is disciplined, awake, and *chaos* is acceptance of the energy that happens within that realm.

STUDENT: You seem to be describing the situation of one person in relation to the space around him or her. I was wondering at what point in our discussion of mandala we are going to talk about reciprocity, interaction. I'm talking about, instead of waiting for later when things will be transmuted, seeing that they are already transmuted.

TRUNGPA RINPOCHE: That's a question of how much you are willing to give in as opposed to wanting to learn something out of this. When you want to learn something out of it, that is very fishy. You have an ulterior motive of wanting to do something with your learning that automatically puts the whole thing off balance. If you are willing to just give in without learning, if you are willing to become rather than learn, that clears the air entirely. At that point, the whole thing becomes a total expression of freedom rather than a student situation. You see, when you want to learn something out of it, you are relating to knowledge as something other than you. When you are willing to *be* with the situation— when you don't give a shit whether you learn or not but you want to be in what is. . . . That is very difficult, but it is very simple at the same time.

S: It seems to me that you have to start by learning, because you are not able to just be right away. If you start by learning, there's some chance to develop an intuitive feeling of things. Then you might be able to just be at that point.

TR: The question is whether you regard learning as something extraordinarily precious or as just something matter-of-fact. You could have the matter-of-fact attitude at the beginning as well. Then you would not have the attitude of being starved, therefore dealing with knowledge as a foreign element coming to you, feeling that knowledge is coming to you and you have to take the whole thing preciously. Instead, as much as possible, you can relate to the whole thing experientially. That way learning becomes matter-of-fact rather than extraordinary.

STUDENT: Where does faith come in?

TRUNGPA RINPOCHE: I suppose in this case faith is the whole approach. If you have faith in yourself as a working basis in a very basic way, you feel that you can handle this whole process. If you don't have faith in yourself, then your relationship to the path becomes living in a myth.

STUDENT: I still don't understand why we have to talk about the five principles from the point of view of a witness. Why can't we talk about it in terms of ourselves?

TRUNGPA RINPOCHE: You are relating with your projections anyway. In any case, you need a formula in your head in terms of language, which automatically means this as opposed to that. So seeing it from the point of view of the other amounts to the same thing.

4

The Watcher's Game

There seems to be more to the five types of samsaric patterns than five heavy-handed styles of existence that are unrelated to each other. The question arises as to how and why these five types of eccentricity occur. This is very important to know, not from the point of view of how to solve the problem, but rather from the point of view of understanding why and how things function together as part of the mandala situation. We are not looking at this whole situation with the idea of getting rid of the problem, because it is an inescapable situation. We cannot get rid of it. It seems to be deep-rooted and completely ingrained in our individual styles. So at this point, I would like to present the active force that relates with basic being and with the five samsaric principles.

The basic being we are discussing here has an element of clarity to it. This is clarity in the sense of not expecting anything at all, just waiting to relate with the next situation. But along with that clarity, there is also a sense of security that would like to capture something, make a record out of the whole situation, make it into a workable situation from the point of view of maintaining ego's existence. That work-

able situation that we deliberately manufacture out of nothing-
ness, out of the open-minded situation, is known as watcher.

We are not satisfied with ourselves and therefore we try our
best to satisfy ourselves, which is the activity of the watcher.
It is a self-defined, dead-end way of surviving. In order to
maintain ourselves, we keep track of the limitations of that
maintenance, and because we know the limitations of that
maintenance, we try to maintain something more. It is a
constant, ongoing situation almost like that of fighting death.
We might know that death is coming very soon, that it is very
close, but still we do not accept death; somehow we try to
make a living out of death itself. In fact we could say that the
whole samsaric structure, samsara and its seductions, is based
on making something eternal out of something impermanent
and transitory. Things are transitory—they cease to exist
because they have been born. But by a twist of logic, we come
to the conclusion that this transitoriness is happening all the
time, and we try to make the transitoriness into eternity. In
the Buddhist tradition, we do not talk about the soul as a
continuing entity. The reason we do not is that it would be
the ultimate hypocrisy—believing in nonexistence as something that exists, believing in transitoriness as something that
is continuous. And that is watcher. The watcher validates its
existence out of falsity; it tries to manufacture falsity as truth.

Believing in eternity seems to be the core of the matter for
watcher and for the five aspects of the samsaric mandala
altogether. We see the texture of vajra aggression or the texture
of ratna richness. In order to maintain that texture and prove
that there is something happening, we have to develop a
certain way of seeing that texture. It consists of gaps, unconditioned gaps, and conditioned points. It is like an enlarged
photograph in which you can begin to see the grain of the
film. Both the grains and the space in between the grains are
constituents of the photograph. What we try to do is convert

the unconditioned space into conditioned dots or points. And we each have our own style of doing that, of looking at things that way. There is the aggression of the vajra family, the pride of the ratna family, the passion of the padma family, the jealousy of the karma family, and the stupidity of the buddha family. In whatever style, we try to hang onto *something* out of nothing.

When we talk about "nothing," it is not a matter of wishful thinking—that the confusion really does not exist. Confusion does exist because it does not exist. This needs very, very careful thinking. Things are as they are because we want them to be that way, and the reason why they are that way is because we feel possibilities of their not being that way. In other words, when we see from the point of view of ego this unconditioned space that we have been talking about, it brings the fear of losing our ground. It is primordial ground that has nothing in it whatsoever that could make it conditioned. And because of that, we find some way of distorting the truth into something that we can hang onto.

This is extremely subtle and basic. In fact, this is the whole way that we distort nirvana into samsara (rather than that samsara and nirvana stand opposed to each other as polarities). In this way, our whole approach becomes very neurotic, almost to the point of schizophrenia. The whole problem arises from looking for a handle, for crutches, for a point of reference to prove that we do exist. By doing that, we come up with our own styles: vajralike, ratnalike, and so on. All these things that we put out are the handle that we want to hang something on. We would like to be saved. We would like to prove our existence by presenting one of those five basic principles.

So this experience of the [conditioned/unconditioned] texture is the experience of watcher, and that is the vital life force of the samsaric mandala. This experience works like this: You have projections and a projector set up, and both projections and projector work together to try to point out their own existence as a valid thing. So each situation confirms its own existence. Projections exist, because the projector has its definite ideas, and the projections prove that the projector is valid, and so forth. In this way, the whole game of the samsaric mandala is the most gigantic syndicate of hypocrisy that ever could be thought of. It has thought itself out, developed its own scheme spontaneously. It is just ape instinct, but it is on an extraordinarily large scale, so large that we can run the whole world on the basis of it—not just this globe, but the entire universe. This scheme is outrageous. It is so outrageous that it is inspiring. It is inspiring that a limited mind could extend itself into limitlessness; it is absurd, but it still does exist. And of course this limited mind is able to give birth to the nirvanic notion of mandala as well. Because of this watcher, because of this hypocrisy and deception, other alternatives begin to create themselves, which we are going to discuss later. The point now is to expose the hypocrisy, expose the game, so that at least the game becomes clear and obvious, a workable situation.

STUDENT: What's the difference between the watcher and the disciplined spontaneity you spoke of in connection with the previous talk?

TRUNGPA RINPOCHE: In the case of watcher, there is always a sense of referring to the end result. You evaluate each step, each move. In spontaneous discipline, you do not care about the end result; it exists because of its own basic situation.

STUDENT: You talked about very careful thinking going into creating the confusion. Could you say more about what that careful thinking is?

TRUNGPA RINPOCHE: Yes, it is true that confusion is

made up of well-thought-out patterns. Confusion is well thought out in order to hypnotize itself. You don't get confused just because your plan is chaotic. You mean to bring about chaos. It is a political move. The purpose is for confusion to perpetuate its own mentality, its own identity. You put out certain ideas in a deliberate attempt to shield yourself from the embarrassment of your own hypocrisy, which has become very comfortable. You develop a pattern of doing continual double-takes with regard to the productions of that hypocrisy. You say, "Oh, that's not a good one," or "That is a good one; let's get into it further." Then the hypocrisy or confusion becomes very solid and definite, and because of that definiteness, you begin to find it very homey. Whenever there is a doubt, you can always go back to that original game. By reflecting back to the original game, you get complete security out of it, you get completely hypnotized by it. Then you can "spontaneously" go on perpetually that way.

S: Why do we create this hypocrisy? So that we can give birth to the mandala?

TR: It's like a mother who doesn't want to go through the pain of giving birth. Each time there is a labor pain, she decides to try not to give birth, to keep the baby inside her womb. She would rather maintain that state constantly, because it is more self-snug, more comfortable. We do it purely for the sake of pleasure, because we don't want to give anything out. It is holding back in that sense. Consequently, we keep continuing on with this baby of ours. It makes us feel secure; it means a lot to us. It makes us feel important, because we are holding another person's life. At the same time, we feel threatened, because another labor pain might come along at any time. Because of that panic, again and again we try to maintain ourselves. We do our best not to give birth to enlightened mind, which is very terrifying and painful. We would have to pass something from us, really give something, and we don't really want to surrender to that degree. We don't really want to have to accept giving something. We don't want to let the product of our work become something outside of us; we don't want to cut the umbilical cord. We would rather preserve it.

S: I don't really see that this is comfortable. It seems uncomfortable.

TR: Well, that depends on how you look at it.

STUDENT: Rinpoche, in the first lecture, you discussed establishing a boundary to a space that we solidify by calling it mine. Is that boundary the rim of the mandala?

TRUNGPA RINPOCHE: Any kind of doubt could be said to be the rim. But the question is whether you want to have the rim, or boundary, as space or freeze it into something solid. In the analogy of hesitating to give birth, in the moment of that hesitation, you are freezing the boundary into something solid so that you get perpetual protection from giving birth.

S: So the boundary of the samsaric mandala is where it fails or falls apart.

TR: Yes.

S: It's its limits.

TR: It is the point of hypocrisy.

STUDENT: How do you deal with the pain of giving birth?

TRUNGPA RINPOCHE: You see, at this point we are not discussing how to deal with the pain, but we are trying to emphasize that the pain does exist. We cannot deal with the pain at all unless we know the nature of the pain and are familiar with its horrific aspect, the imprisonment aspect of the pain. How to deal with it seems to be unnecessary or unimportant. In fact, the problem all along in the past has been that too many ideas have been presented on how you can save yourself rather than on why you should save yourself or what the problem actually is. So at this point, we are discussing the heavy-handedness of the whole thing, rather than how we can be saved, which comes spontaneously. Once you know the nature of the heavy-handedness, the rest is obvious. We have no trouble getting out of it at all. That happens spontaneously.

S: The pain is not wanting to let go?

TR: Yes. You don't want to give birth or go as far as cutting the umbilical cord. The fear is that in giving birth and cutting the umbilical cord, you will become an insignificant person. From the point of cutting the umbilical cord, your child will grow up and become independent of you, another entity. Later on, you will become an insignificant person. We don't want to go through that; in fact, we become resentful about it.

S: It seems to be exactly the same as not wanting to die.

TR: That's right, precisely. Creating another entity means that you become an insignificant person. One day people will refer to your son or daughter as somebody else having nothing to do with you. At the most, they might be kind enough to say his father or mother is so-and-so, rather than speaking about your son. So there is that fear that you will become something insignificant in the background.

STUDENT: Is there anything that can be said about the incredible power of samsara? There are all those things that make it difficult to give birth, which make it difficult to see the hypocrisy, accept the hypocrisy, maybe work with the hypocrisy. Why is it so horrible, so incredibly . . .

TRUNGPA RINPOCHE: I think you are beginning to speak sense. You are quite right. Why? Why on earth? That's like a mantra. It's like Ramana Maharshi's teaching of "Who am I?" If you regard that as a question, then you miss the point. "Who am I?" in your practice of meditation should be regarded as a statement. If we regard "Who am I" as a statement, then we begin to open something. Why, why, why. Then you are not starved, but have already become rich.

There are two kinds of approaches. "Why" as a question is an expression of starvation. "Why" as a statement expresses the mentality of richness. In other words, if you regard it as an embryonic question concerning how the whole thing begins, it provides a lot of space rather than hunger. Space is not hungry; space is self-contained. It is rich already, because it has its own space. It has the space to afford to be space, spaciousness.

This is a very good point, which we can expand on as we continue.

5

The Lubrication of Samsara

I feel that we have not yet discussed the samsaric aspect of mandala enough to get the general feel of it. In spite of not having much time left, we might still have to go into it further. It is worthwhile spending more time on confusion. Talking about confusion is much more helpful than talking about how to save ourselves. Once we know what to be saved from and what not to be saved from, then the rest becomes obvious. The general pattern of American karma as well as of the American approach to spirituality is another element that causes us to emphasize our confusion rather than purely making promises. Making promises tends to encourage spiritual materialism, which is an involvement with wanting to be saved rather than an understanding of what there is to be saved from. The tendency toward spiritual materialism is by far the most powerful one at hand, and we do not want to encourage an already aggravated situation such as that.

In terms of the samsaric mandala, there is something further that we have not yet discussed that lubricates the confusion and makes it functional and flowing. The basic nature of the samsaric mandala is comprised of anger, pride, passion, jealousy, and ignorance. But looking at the totality of samsara in those terms alone is very crude. There's something far more subtle than that.

We have already discussed experiencing the texture of situations and the deceptive way of looking at things that is connected with that. There are also mixed feelings involved with this—a sense of sanity and insanity at the same time. But what we want to discuss now is more fundamental. It goes back to the basic area we discussed right at the beginning of the seminar when we talked about solid space and spacious boundary and spacious space and solid boundary. Somehow that is what provides the fundamental situation.

What is it that causes the samsaric communication of aggression to passion, passion to ignorance, ignorance to pride, and so forth? What is it that causes that to keep communicating itself to itself? What causes the survival of those five principles that we have discussed, including the experiencing of the texture? Why do they keep surviving? If they are solid blocks of neurosis, why don't they self-destruct? A state of anger and aggression feeds itself and destroys itself. Ignorance feeds itself by ignoring everything, but in the end there's no outlet, no way of relating to anything in the world outside, so it should diminish by itself. So what is it that keeps these emotions functioning as they seem to in the real world of samsara that we live in?

The pattern that develops that keeps up and maintains the whole environment of samsaric confusion has something to do with totality. There is something total happening. There is a totality of frivolousness, a totality of looking for entertainment, and a totality comprised of seeking survival through all-pervasive aggression. Those three principles seem to function simultaneously on the level of the totality to keep the individual qualities of confused mind alive. The individual characteristics of confused mind can be kept alive because there is a sympathetic environment functioning, which could be composed of two, three, four, or five of the confused states of mind that exist. So what we are pointing to here is the sympathetic environment that we tend to create rather than just to the five heavy-handed emotions as such. That sympathetic environment could be based on frivolousness, to take as an example one situation that is very prevalent right now.

Frivolousness is an area in which there is a sense of all-pervasiveness, but there are little particles jumping back and forth within that all-pervasive space. The space is uncertainty, and the particles are inquisitive mind. Those two form the totality of frivolousness, the totality of the frivolous sympathetic environment.

Frivolousness in this case is quite different from the ordinary popular idea of being silly or childish. There can be sophisticated frivolousness, frivolousness that is based on a cynical attitude toward traditions that have developed, toward the patterns that have formed in our society. With this attitude, we feel up-to-date. We feel we are justified in criticizing or being cynical toward the existing pattern.

We have telephone poles with wires strung between them; we have the pattern of breakfast, lunch, and dinner that we have to conform with; people keep their front lawns neat with lawn mowers—these are broad basic patterns. Society functions in a certain way based on inspirations of the past. Certain patterns have been passed down by people from generation to generation that make it possible to keep society alive, to keep it neat and tidy and clean and functional. These things have nothing at all to do with philosophy or ecology. They take place on a simple, straightforward level—there's a rock, there's a tree, there's grass growing, there's a sky, there's a sunset.

We could criticize the sunset, saying, "This looks like a postcard picture." That is a perfect example of frivolous cynicism. We criticize people saying that so-and-so acts just like a typical grandfather or father or brother or mother-in-law. We tend to make certain assumptions and develop our cynical approach on the basis of them. It is as though the whole environment is totally poisoned. Whatever landmarks exist—telephone poles with wires running between them, neatly cut lawns, and so on—we use as targets.

What we seem to be discussing here is the frivolousness of the "avant-garde," which everybody thinks they are somehow associated with. We think that we are progressive and transformed people. We have a different perspective on society, which *they* have fucked up for us. We are resentful about that, and that makes us the avant-garde. We are the messengers of a new age, the Aquarian age, or whatever you call it. It is antitradition, anti-establishment, obviously. In fact, we could say it is anti-earth, because the earth has had to be cultivated, and cities have had to be built on it, so now we are resentful about the earth.

I'm not particularly condemning being resentful of pollution. There is nothing cynical about that. That problem arises to begin with because we regard the whole world just as a gigantic world of opportunity for us in which we can build up our own kind of cynicism and unfriendliness. We can make the whole world into a gigantic satire. But by taking that satirical approach, we are pulling the rug out from under our own feet. The detrimental result of such an approach is that people end up by killing themselves, or for that matter, laughing their heads off. Those two extremes do arise.

The whole cynical approach is an extraordinarily aggressive one. The joke that develops out of it is a pointed joke, an aggressive joke. It is making fun of somebody's thousand years of accomplishment, which is tradition. Tradition, whether developed in the East or the West, is not particularly a laughing matter, because people meant it. We could say that it is too heavy, not light enough, but so what? We do not have to reduce that ground to frivolousness, reduce it to our satirical or hysterical approach.

What I'm trying to say is that we have a very glib and easy way of pointing out the negative situations and the situations that are prone to cynicism, the humorous situations of spiritual and psychological materialism. We criticize how people run their businesses and how they drive themselves mad, and how they run their so-called enlightened society. In doing that, we do not leave any room—any freedom—to be inspired, which is something that does happen constantly at the same time as being critical. The fact that we do not leave that room does not mean that there isn't any. There is tremendous room for psychological materialism and its businesslike, economic approach, and there is tremendous room at the same time for tradition that has nothing at all to do with psychological or spiritual materialism. And there is also room to appreciate the existing patterns that have already been created, which—of course—are a mishmash of spiritual materialism and genuine spirituality, both at the same time.

The point is that it is easy to criticize the materialistic approach, both psychological and spiritual, and to destroy it logically. But the real problem that we have to face is putting ourselves in the same boat as those we are criticizing, as if *we* had to take responsibility for running the whole world economically, spiritually, psychologically, and politically. How would we do it? That seems to be the real problem.

The frivolousness that goes on in ego's mentality has intelligence in it as well, which communicates back and forth between aggression and passion and so on. But at the same time, it has an extraordinarily resentful quality. It blames. It says, "It's somebody else's fault, therefore I have nothing to do with it. *My* duty, my life's occupation, is to make fun of other people constantly, to regard them as a big joke, to regard the whole world as a big joke."

This is quite a different big joke from the one that developed in the tantric tradition. Maya, or illusion, the dance of the dakinis, is also a big joke.[1] But it is not a cynical joke. It is a serious joke, if I may say so. The difference between a cynical joke and a serious joke is a very interesting one. The cynical joke is much more heavy-handed than the enlightened ones. The enlightened jokes are much lighter, because they leave room to accept wisdom, to accept the past.

Take Naropa, for example. He spent twelve years going through all kinds of painful tortures imposed by his guru Tilopa, and he attained the level of a lineage holder of the Kagyü tradition. And that is the path that we now have here. That is what we have to hold onto. It was not a joke; it was not a game. It was a matter of consequence. On the other hand, the kind of approach that regards everything as unreal because that provides a way to escape from it is the lubrication that has developed in the samsaric mandala. That disregarding of the effort and energy put in by people in the past goes on all the time.

Of course we might object, saying, "I don't want to be dogmatic," "I don't want to be a convert," "I don't want to be a heavy person," or "I don't want to trip out about anything at all." But all that "I don't want to, I don't want to, I don't want to" is itself an extremely heavy trip. We are trying to put ourselves in an extremely safe situation in which there is no room for committing ourselves to a tradition, no room for relating to any solid ground at all. We might say that the ascetic trip of Milarepa was too pure, or Naropa's approach of having visions and trying to follow them was very psychedelic and trippy. And, we might say, Tilopa was the greatest tripper of them all. There is no end to our cynicism. We do not allow any kind of space or room to move about with the dignity of basic tradition. We alienate ourselves from the inheritance that we have received and from the work that other people have put into society to produce this particular kind of solid situation. This is one of the plagues that could develop from taking a cynical attitude toward spirituality, even spiritual materialism. A very powerful, widespread disease of this type could develop.

That approach of trying to establish your ground somewhere but nowhere, which lubricates the situations of ego and its constituents of passion, pride, aggression, and so forth, goes on all the time. It is an approach of carelessness, of feeling that everything is going to be okay because we are allied with a super-satire person, a supercynic. "If there are any kind of trips going on with something wrong in them, my satirical authority figure is going to see it and transmit the message to me." As a result of this kind of attitude, we end up having nothing—just an extremely frivolous situation.

The whole point is that what lubricates the samsaric mandala is a frivolous approach to samsara—not taking samsara's game seriously enough. We fail to regard samsara as something very powerful, very energetic. We tend to dismiss it as belonging to an area of mistake, not realizing that the mistake has been made seriously and meaningfully. Such mistakes bring about the sacrifice of many lives and a great deal of time. They are monuments. So samsara is a very monumental situation rather than something frivolous. Somebody decides to do it; it is not an accident. It is not something frivolous, it is a very serious game. We have to learn to respect the monumental creation called samsara. It is because of its monumental quality that it also breeds nirvana at the same time, as a by-the-way situation. So we cannot purely take a satirical approach toward samsara. We have to take it very seriously and the whole world very seriously. This seems to be a very important point.

STUDENT: Is this kind of lubrication found only in the West?

TRUNGPA RINPOCHE: I think it is found everywhere. It happens in the East as well, or anywhere where a highly traditional society decides to do something insane and is criticized and laughed at. It is found all over the globe and even among Martians!

S: How do you deal with it if it's so monumental? How do you get through it if you want to respect it and everything that went into it but still don't want to go along with it?

TR: It is such a monumental situation that you respect it for that. It is extraordinary, impressive; it is extraordinarily documentary. You respect it as a landmark. If you do that, what we talked about right at the beginning of the seminar can happen: you can begin to realize that space happens within those monumental things and becomes more significant than the monuments themselves. The monuments—the Statues of Liberty—are hollow monuments. But until you realize the monumental quality of the Statue of Liberty, you don't see all that it is. You have to respect things; in other words, the whole thing is regarded as sacred.

STUDENT: I'm cynical.

TRUNGPA RINPOCHE: Okay.

S: But I also have a tendency to be too serious. I can't seem to really understand what it is to have a sense of humor. So part of my being cynical is wanting to have a sense of humor. It comes out in cynicism.

TR: How would you develop your sense of humor?

S: Maybe you can't develop it?

TR: How do you develop your seriousness?

S: By being too attached, too worried about myself.

TR: How about the space between the two [between humor and seriousness]? What happens there, can you tell me?

S: [Student is unable to answer.]

TR: I think that is the interesting area. It is not so important what happens in terms of that and this, but what happens in between the two.

STUDENT: The tradition here seems to be a tradition of forced change, constant innovation. If we go along with that, we find ourselves with changes that are very unpleasant for the entire globe. Many of us are here at this seminar perhaps because of a recognition that we have to return to the sources of a genuine tradition that is monumental . . .

TRUNGPA RINPOCHE: We are talking about monumental in the sense of solid space or hollow space. We are not talking about *the* monument or *the* landmark that is connected with the dharmakaya or dharmadhatu realm.[2] That is very different—

S: It's very different from the mentality that has created the H-bomb and is destroying the globe ecologically. For me it's not a matter of resenting tradition as much as of having to reject it out of the same source from which I recognize humanity in myself and my relation to the whole biosphere, all living things. I must reject a cultural tradition that tends to destroy that relatedness.

TR: Well, that's some kind of respect, isn't it?

S: Well, I don't feel cynical, but I do have to reject what I see in the cultural tradition.

TR: In other words, you have to reject not being a poet. Do you write poetry?

S: Yes.

TR: You do? How? What line do you take in relating to the world in the realm of poetry? How do you write poetry so that it doesn't become solid?

S: On the basis of what you've said about mandalas, I would say that my conception of a poem is a mandala. It's a recognition of a bounded area, and one of the limitations of that is that it's words. Is that what you mean?

TR: Not exactly. The idea is that poetry could become hollow poetry, like a concretized sponge. It has the stoneness or rocklike quality of concrete, but at the same time it's filled with all kinds of space. Consequently, if you threw it in the water, it would float, rather than sinking to the bottom of the pond.

S: It seems to me that avant-garde cynicism gets to be a tradition in itself.

TR: That's true. For instance, the early poems of Allen Ginsberg and a lot of poets and playwrights of the American Beat Generation are very satirical about society. And in particular, a lot of inspiration sprung up after the Vietnam War, which provided something to work with in terms of basic material. There is nothing particularly wrong with the satirical remarks or satirical poems themselves at all. They're beautiful. They see all kinds of areas, all kinds of corners. They speak beautifully. But what is the matter with that poetry is the punctuation, which speaks of mutual embarrassment. Nobody talks about freeing ourselves from the hysterical entrapment we have been discussing here. So something is unsaid, remains unsaid all the time, whenever we criticize. That unspeakable truth becomes haunting—like the ghost of George Washington! It's all over.

S: How does what you're saying relate to exposing the hypocrisy of the samsaric mandala?

TR: We have to acknowledge that to begin with. We are not advanced enough to expose it as a matter of public humiliation. At this point we're merely concerned with acknowledging that such a thing is happening and with digging it out from the subconscious or unconscious embarrassment that keeps us wanting to keep silent about that whole area.

S: Does the mandala have a historic aspect? Is there a forward and backward?

TR: Mandala is time in its own way, so obviously future and past become the mandala.

S: Can we see it going forward?

TR: As well as coming backward.

S: Where would the viewer be standing in relation to that?

TR: Nowhere.

STUDENT: I don't understand what you mean by lubricating the samsaric mandala. You said frivolousness lubricates it.

TRUNGPA RINPOCHE: I mean lubrication in a pejorative sense.

S: It makes it more slippery?

TR: It provides a slippery situation so you can sneak in and out without being caught.

S: In other words, so we don't have to deal with—

TR: So you don't have to deal with reality.

S: When you were talking about respecting the monument, did you mean in the sense of respecting the power of an enemy? Since so many lives have fallen to this monumental tradition, it's not something just to laugh off and dismiss frivolously, but should be respected as something that has taken many human lives?

TR: Respecting it as an enemy or not as an enemy amounts to the same thing. It is both the irritatingly common enemy and a source of wisdom at the same time—because it is a landmark of that as opposed to this.

S: Let us take the example of well-manicured lawns. I can see how the satirical response to that definitely leaves something unsaid. But on the other hand, if you're respecting that situation, doesn't that leave the scorn unsaid? Isn't that appropriate also—your scorn or distaste for that?

TR: I wouldn't say that all of it is appropriate. There is unsaid space all over the situation, which could be called stagnation from ego's point of view. In terms of ego's mandala, it is stagnation. There is stagnation as well as space within the stagnation, which is worth looking at. What I have been saying is that there is no solution, really, and there is no absence of a solution, really, either. The point is to find that area where both a solution and the solutionless situation can function simultaneously. Find that space. Space doesn't provide either birth or death. There is something total, something happening as a totality. So the problems and the possibilities of the samsaric mandala can function simultaneously.

STUDENT: I would like to find some space in guilt. What is the position of guilt in the mandala?

TRUNGPA RINPOCHE: That you feel terribly guilty that you have created the mandala. At the same time, you have created that guilt, which is itself space. That is to say, you never necessarily had to create the mandala; you needn't have started the mandala at all. So guilt goes both ways. There is guilt related to having made mistakes and there is guilt as the working basis. From that point of view, nobody is punished and nobody is confirmed. I'm afraid the answer does not come out very straightforward. The answer is only food for your further understanding.

STUDENT: What part does fear play in all this?

TRUNGPA RINPOCHE: Fear is the antilubricational aspect

of the samsaric mandala as well as a lubricator at the same time. Fear is about how things might happen and also about how they might *not* work. It goes both ways at the same time. It's like the symbolism of the vajra. It has a ball in the middle, which joins the two ends. The ball in the middle represents space, and things going on at the two ends are the energy of fear. This end might work or possibly that end might work. But both ends are related to the central area in which we have to give up that particular trip altogether.

S: What about somebody who completely believes in tradition and lives their whole life according to it? Still they have passion, aggression, ignorance, and fear going on, because they're dead serious.

TR: That is automatically antitraditional. That's not realizing what tradition actually means.

STUDENT: Rinpoche, could you say something about the other two of the three lubricants you mentioned: entertainment and aggression?

TRUNGPA RINPOCHE: I think there is no point in going into great detail on those. The whole point is that they create some kind of excuse, and the way of doing that is to create a link within the space—some kind of circulation. It is like the veins and arteries that keep up the circulation while the basic body is functioning. One can imagine how it works: all kinds of little discursive thoughts, little games going on constantly, either trying to grasp what is happening or trying to escape from it, or else trying to relax between the two. The point is that that kind of mind is going on all the time, and it is lubrication rather than a basic principle like, for example, the five basic principles that we discussed. It is intermediary in relation to all those situations. This is the case with frivolousness and a cynical attitude toward the world, toward life, toward poetry, art, and so on.

6

Totality

The samsaric mandala provides energy beyond the samsaric level. When we say "beyond," the idea is not of getting out of samsara, or even, for that matter, of transcending it in the ordinary sense. We are talking about getting to the source of the samsaric mandala, to the background of it. We are talking about a way in more than about a way out. This is because the nature of the samsaric mandala contains within it nonduality, absence of confusion, and freedom. In other words, being able to see the source, or background, of the samsaric mandala is the mandala of freedom.

In the beginning of the seminar, we talked about solid space and a spacious fringe. From our present point of view, neither the space nor the solidity are a part of the buddha mandala; rather it is the total situation in which those two polarities can exist and maintain themselves. The buddha mandala is a kind of environment or air in which the two polarities can maintain themselves. So we are not so much discussing liberation from samsaric confusion, but we are looking at the ground in which both liberation and confusion can maintain themselves and also dissolve.

Liberation and confusion are seen in terms of a mandala

pattern, but in that mandala pattern, realization and confusion are still interdependent, still conditioned. Therefore, even freedom or spaciousness or goodness is also part of the samsaric mandala along with wickedness (or whatever you want to call it). So we are not discussing a war between samsara and nirvana and considering how one of them could defeat or overcome the other. We are discussing the environment in which the energy of those two can exist and maintain itself. We are talking about the energy that gives birth and brings death at the same time, that totality on its own absolute level, without watcher, without observer. This is the idea of _dharmata,_ which means "that which is," "being in itself," or "constantly being."

These ideas may seem quite abstract if we just look at them from this angle, but we can also look at them on the practical level of our day-to-day lives. For instance, we can see our aggression and passion or conventional goodness, piety, and love. We can see how all those things function in a kind of basic totality. We have the possibility of anger, of passion, and of ignorance—these emotions have to function somewhere. They draw energy out and redistribute it and draw it out again. A complete cycle, or circulation, takes place. That which provides the possibility for such a circulation to take place is the basic totality that we are talking about—dharmata.

This could hardly be said to be connected only with nirvana—that would be a one-sided view. In a totally awake situation, emotions arise and develop, but those emotions have unconditioned qualities in them. In that sense, the emotions have their polarities and dichotomies.

In actual practice, we might express our aggression, our anger, by hitting someone or destroying someone or by being verbally nasty. Such actions and frustrations coming out of our emotions are the result of failing to realize that there is a total space in which these energies are functioning. In other words, suppressing or acting out both produce substitute emotions rather than true emotions. Both are sedatives. Experiencing perfect, or true, emotions means realizing the background totality, realizing that the emotions are functioning or happening in the midst of a whole space. At that point, we begin to experience the flavors of the emotions, their textures, their temperatures. We begin to feel the living aspect of the emotions rather than the frustrated aspect.

What frustration means in this context is stagnation—we want to give birth but we cannot. Therefore, we scream, we try to push out, we try to burst out. We feel that though something is definitely happening, still something is not quite there. There is a sense of "unaccomplishment," a sense of something being totally wrong on the emotional level. This is because we fail to see the totality, the whole, which is the mandala principle. We could call this the buddha mandala. I prefer not to use the term *mandala of nirvana,* because it has an element of dichotomy (the war between samsara and nirvana) in it.

This does not refer only to emotions but applies to our daily-life experience as a whole. Once we see the totality, we have the experience of seeing things as they are in their own fullest sense. The blueness of the sky and the greenness of the fields do not need confirmation, and they also do not need a sense of extraordinary appreciation. They are *so,* therefore we do not have to be reassured that they are so. When we realize the basic totality of the whole situation, then perceptions become extraordinarily vivid and precise. This is because they are not colored by the fundamental conventionality of believing in something. In other words, when there's no dogma— when there's no belief in the blueness of the sky and the greenness of the field—then we begin to see the totality. The reason why perceptions are much more spectacular and colorful then is that we do not transmit the message of duality between solidity and spaciousness. Such a message is transmitted when we fail to see the sharp edges of things precisely. If we experience solid space and hollow grass, at that very boundary where the space meets the grass, a faint message is interchanged. It is like the border guards of two countries exchanging cigarettes with each other. There is a fuzzy edge there. It is not black and white, not precise.

That same thing happens if we decide to give up samsara and try to associate ourselves with nirvana. The journey from samsara's area automatically brings a sense of the past. There is the sense of making a journey into some other realm. In this case the other realm is nirvana, or goodness, or whatever you would like to call it. The sense of achieving this journey in itself becomes an expression of samsara or hangup, because you are still involved with directions [still biased in favor of one of the two polarities]. That's why there's no black-and-white world. As far as the dualistic world of samsara and nirvana is concerned, until one is able to relate to the total basic mandala, faint exchanges continue to take place. Nothing is seen precisely and clearly. Before you see black as black and white as white, there is a grayness, a very faint and subtle grayness of communication across the borderline between black and white.

This is of course what we were talking about earlier when we were discussing frivolousness and when we were discussing the sense of security and discursive thoughts or metaphysical, philosophical concepts. Here there are no definite metaphysical, philosophical concepts or definite emotions, but there is [still the sense of duality], something that is like the smell in a broken perfume bottle. It still contains some awareness that there was perfume in it, although there is nothing in it anymore.

From the point of view of the awakened state of mind, the

basic mandala does not require transmission of any lineal messages in order to see things as they are.[1] That is why the tantric tradition speaks of transmutation. The characteristic of transmutation is that lead is changed *completely* into gold, absolutely pure gold without a trace of lead. The lead is totally and completely changed. It is a black-and-white situation.

The idea of a leap, or jump, has been mentioned in this connection in the traditional books. But what is involved here is not really a leap or jump. If we use those terms, the whole principle might be misinterpreted once again in the sense of a journey forward. There is a particular Tibetan term that is appropriate here: *la da wa* or *la da*. *La* means the top of the ridge in a mountain pass; *dawa* means "gone beyond it." You don't just go beyond the ridge, you go beyond ridgeness itself. In other words, you don't leap forward; rather, in making the necessary preparations for leaping, you realize that there is no need to leap forward, but you have already arrived by leaping backward. You find that the carpet has already been pulled out from under your feet, so at that point, the journey becomes unnecessary. The notion of leap itself becomes unnecessary. If you have a "leap," that is an idea or concept. That is walking on solid space.

At this point, we might find the basic totality of the mandala extremely terrifying. There is no ground, there is no journey, there is not even any effort. We cannot even deny it, because we discover it. And we cannot put it into terms or ideas. The self-destructive situation of ego simultaneously finds its self-creative situation.

In that sense, the totality of the mandala brings basic unification. This unification comes in the five parts that we have already discussed in terms of the samsaric mandala—the four types of samsaric setups plus the one in the middle. But before we get into the details of those in terms of the buddha mandala, I would like to make sure that everybody knows, as far as words and concepts can convey, that what we are discussing is not so much structures or qualities or diagrams or interrelatedness at all. What we are discussing at this point is complete totality that does not depend on its expressions or manifestations or anything. It is *whole,* because the space and the boundary are always simultaneously there, everywhere. It does not need any journey or relationships. This acts as the sustainer of confusion, samsara, as well as of its counterpart nirvana with its inspiration. This process of the basic mandala is simultaneously death and birth. It is creative as well as destructive at the same time, in every single moment, fraction of a second, or whatever you would like to call it—beyond time and space. There is no time and space, because there is no polarity. If there is no polarity, then it happens at once. That is why there is no room for conceptualization. When you formulate concepts you give birth, and then that which you gave birth to undergoes old age and begins to die. But here, no such lineal journey is involved.

This situation is described in certain tantric texts as *sang thal,* which means in Tibetan "transparent," or "simultaneously penetrating." This does not mean transparent from somebody else's point of view, as though someone is standing behind a glass window; but it is from the point of view of the glass window itself. That is the way it is transparent. It doesn't need watcher anymore, because it is transparent by itself.

All these ideas of the basic mandala, the total mandala, that we have been discussing are on the whole from nobody's point of view. The mandala is its own point of view. Therefore, it is free from birth and death as well as being the epitome of birth and death at the same time. It is that which sustains the whole universe, the whole of existence, as well as that which kills everything. In the tantric tradition, it is often referred to as the charnel ground. In the iconography of the charnel ground, there is the sage of the charnel ground, the river of the charnel ground, the tree of the charnel ground, and the pagoda of the charnel ground. This iconography is the expression that birth and death takes place there simultaneously. There are skeletons dancing and wild animals tearing apart bodies. Somebody else chases the animals and they drop the bodies. There are loose legs, loose arms, and loose heads. While one wild animal is chewing one part of a body, another more powerful animal comes and eats its tail. By trying to run away from death, it simultaneously creates it. It is very gloomy and terrifying—nothing pleasant, particularly. If you look at it from somebody else's point of view, it becomes extraordinarily unpleasant. But from its own point of view it is self-existing, extremely rich and fertile.

STUDENT: Is the center of the wheel of life the charnel ground?

TRUNGPA RINPOCHE: No, I wouldn't say that. That would be more Yama himself, who carries the wheel of life and is birth and death simultaneously.[2] It is the whole totality rather than the source of energy. It is the situation in which energy can exist rather than a particular point within that or a particular relational action.

STUDENT: Is it possible to have a vague experience of this totality? It seems as though there is some kind of feeling of this totality that exists all the time, but it is very vague because if you try to watch it or grab onto it, it dissolves away.

TRUNGPA RINPOCHE: That is so, because that sense of vagueness is a sense of insecurity. There is a sense that something is wrong, something is not quite right, because fundamentally there is no ground anymore. There's no solidness to dwell on. That is the mystical experience of the ultimate meaning of duhkha, pain, suffering, discomfort. We begin to find the meaninglessness of materialistic pleasure and so on, but there's something more than that: fundamentally, we can feel something and we can't make up our minds whether it is something for us or against us, but there is something going on. That sense that something is cooking could also be described as the experience of buddha-nature, in fact.[3] But we can't put our finger on it or create it.

S: Does the insecurity disappear as you experience it more often?

TR: If you try to make it into a basis for security, then it doesn't exist anymore.

S: Is the idea to try to have an experience that is neutral with regard to samsara and nirvana?

TR: Basically, any form of experience contains a sense of reference point which is the basis for rejecting or accepting. You cannot have experience without painful or pleasurable situations. You cannot just have neutral experience at all. The extreme or biased experiences that you have are part of the chaos. These kinds of chaotic experiences have been systematically arranged in a workable fashion by religious practitioners for the sake of their books, their holy books. They have categorized certain things as good and certain things as bad, associating them with God or Satan. But on the whole we are not discussing which experiences are valid and which are not. Rather we are saying that the whole thing has no substance in it.

S: The comparison has no substance?

TR: Right, because it is dependent on the other point of view.

S: So the point of view is not important either. The vagueness is almost more important than the point of view.

TR: Yes, from the point of view of spaciousness or totality.

S: So it is better to remain vague than define things or take a point of view that needs to be expressed.

TR: I wouldn't say just purely remain vague. But if you remain vague on a very subtle level—not having a reference point—then that vagueness becomes very lively; it becomes luminous in fact. Instead of being vague and gray, it becomes dazzling. It also becomes somewhat definite, but not from the point of view of polarities. It becomes definite in its own innate nature, because there is no watcher involved.

STUDENT: When you talked about the hollow grass and the solid space and the grayness in between, I didn't understand. Perhaps it has to do with this vagueness.

TRUNGPA RINPOCHE: No, that is not this kind of vagueness exactly. That is a kind of deceptive vagueness in which you can't make up your mind. You have to maintain allegiance toward both ends. In other words, you depend on hope as well as on fear, and you want to keep a foot in both camps.

S: You hope that the grass is there and—

TR: And fear that it isn't. But still there is some way of twisting the fear around. It's a very cunning game.

S: So the grayness comes from our own oscillation.

TR: Yes, very much so. Or more likely from a deceptive sense of community, a deceptive attitude of cooperation, coexistence, rather than aloneness.

S: Is that kind of midway between having solid grass and empty space?

TR: Yes.

S: And the third alternative?

TR: A sense of allegiance to somewhere, something. But

that is equally confused. The reason why it is gray is that watching yourself lubricates everything between the hollow space and solid grass—or the other way around, whatever. The commentator makes everything comfortable, so that you don't have to make a sudden entrance into anything. It is like flying from one country that is cold to another one that is hot in an air-conditioned airplane. That makes the situation bearable so that you don't have to go through sudden changes. Everything is made as hospitable as possible.

S: Then the Buddha's state of mind must be very uncomfortable.

TR: Not at all, because there is no watcher. It is being itself.

S: But you said that it's watcher that makes things comfortable.

TR: As well as paranoid at the same time. Watcher intends to make things comfortable.

S: I see.

TR: But the Buddha's mind is not concerned with any of that, so a whole big area is taken away. Economically, it is very cheap.

STUDENT: How can we see the charnel ground in our own experience?

TRUNGPA RINPOCHE: It is the sense of threat that most people experience. You feel that you are on the verge of a freakout and are losing your ground in terms of keeping a grip on who are your enemies and who are your friends. You want to make sure that they are enemies and friends and don't want to confuse the two. You want to make the whole thing definite. That in itself becomes very painful and uninviting. As Buddhists, the whole thing that we are trying to do is to approach an area that nobody wants to get into. People try to run away from it all the time and in that way have created samsara. As long as we are on the path and practicing and developing, we are doing this impossible thing, approaching that thing that people have been rejecting for millions of years. We find it extremely discomfiting, and we are going toward it, exploring it. That is why it is so painful to give and open. That kind of unwanted place is like the charnel ground. It haunts us all over the place, not just one place.

S: It seems to be the state where there's the most possibility for transformation.

TR: Precisely, yes. Needless to say.

STUDENT: Can you say something about the mandala just as a shape, a pattern, rather than as what it contains? I know this is very imprecise, but what makes it so extraordinary to see the whole thing as a mandala rather than as just statements of fact like any other religion or system does?

TRUNGPA RINPOCHE: The point is that one sees the totality, the whole area. One begins to have an extraordinary panoramic vision with no boundaries. One can afford to associate with particular energies, particular directions then, because one's working situation is not based on a sense of direction anymore. You have a directionless direction. It is an entirely new approach to time and space. You can approach time because it is timeless; you can approach space because it is spaceless. There is a direction because there are no directions at the same time. This opens up tremendous possibilities of another way of looking at the whole thing. At the same time, of course, there's no reference point, therefore you can't keep track of it. Wanting to keep track of it would be comparable to wanting to attend one's own funeral.

S: Rinpoche, would it be possible to view the totality of the situation like a field upon which there's a football game. There's this and that—it's like a game between God and the devil, nirvana and samsara. And that panorama sort of has a pointless point of view from the ground position. It sort of shoots God and the devil out of the saddle at the same time.

TR: That's right, yes. That's a good one.

S: Is that prajna?

TR: No, that's jnana.[4] In prajna there's still a watcher. Prajna would be like a panoramic television camera viewing the scene from the point of view of space. Jnana is the point of view of the ground itself.

STUDENT: Rinpoche, it seems to me that in the samsaric mandala, everything is so neatly divided and compartmentalized into five segments with lines or barriers between the segments. Do these barriers refer to anything in terms of the functioning of ego?

TRUNGPA RINPOCHE: They are connected with the watcher—with the sense of intellect or the sense of watcher. We constantly refer back to our central headquarters to make sure everything is functionally lubricated. This is connected with an attitude of being dependent on survival. Our motto is: "We have to survive." In order to survive, we have to do these things, and there is a tremendous threat of death, yet we think that we are constantly creating life. Of course, from another point of view, we are creating death at the same time, so this approach defeats itself.

STUDENT: Rinpoche, you talked about orderly chaos. The orderly aspect was connected with discipline, and the chaos was the energy that is happening at a given point. Was that connected with the approach we are speaking of now, an approach to the total ground in which everything is happening? Is discipline being able to see birth and death simultaneously?

TRUNGPA RINPOCHE: Being in a position to experience orderly chaos is itself the discipline. But then as far as the relationship to orderly chaos is concerned, it is something extraordinarily organic. There is a totality that takes care of the chaos, that puts things into a situation.

S: Do you take care of the discipline or is the discipline already there?

TR: The discipline is already there. On the whole, we could say that discipline is like a refrigerator. The chaos is all the chaotic things going on inside the refrigerator—there are so many things in the refrigerator. The orderliness is that the refrigerator breathes cold air on all of it.

7

The Mandala of Unconditioned Being

Let us continue our discussion of totality, the total space of dharmata. There are different aspects of that basic total space, different aspects of the totality of the basic mandala of unconditioned being. There is an element of accommodation and there is also an element of vastness. Here accommodation becomes energetic, because accommodation is allowing a space to develop or allowing things to develop within a certain space. When trees grow and grass grows, space also takes part in that growth, that energy, at the same time. Without the basic space there cannot be trees or grass or any kind of energy developing.

Accommodation is the aspect of efficiency. The other aspect of the space is a kind of acceptance, the quality of letting things expand to their fullest extent.

In talking about the five buddha principles, we are not saying that they are five definite, individual entities. They are aspects of the basic totality that accommodates things and allows them to happen. So it is not so much a matter of five separate buddha qualities; rather there are five aspects of the totality. We are talking about one situation from five different angles.

So there are these two basic qualities to the totality: the energy or efficiency or accommodation aspect of the space and the expansiveness aspect of it. Those two function on a nondual—not-two—level. This nonduality is a third quality of the totality.

The nondual aspect of the totality is the buddha family, which is constantly accommodating in its own fullest way, unmoved by any particular events. It is symbolized in the traditional iconography by a wheel eternally revolving. It has a sense of timelessness, constant being.

The energy or efficiency aspect is connected with the karma and vajra families. All these distinctions we are making and descriptions of aspects we are giving here are less concerned with what is contained than with the container. Efficiency from this point of view means providing accommodation for efficiency rather than being efficient in the active sense.

There are two ways of instigating efficiency. One is through the sharpness of vajra, which covers all the territory and all the areas, so that, as far as the space is concerned, there are no unsurveyed areas left. Because of that quality of surveying all areas, we could use the word *intellect* here in a relative sense, though it may not apply on the absolute level. We can speak of intellect here in virtue of its precision and sharpness.

The other style of efficiency is karma, which is not efficient so much in the sense of covering all areas as in the sense of believing in automatic fulfillment. There is the sense that things are already being fulfilled, so there is an ongoing energy of total functioning. You don't have to try to function or try to fulfill, because everything is being fulfilled. Because of that, you do not have to push into any particular area. That is karma—seeing the totality of action as it is, so there is no struggle involved.

The acceptance or expansive aspect of dharmata, or total basic space, is connected with padma and ratna. Ratna sees everything in terms of oneness or sameness. In other words, the notion of expanding into a certain territory does not apply anymore, because the space is seen as self-existing. Everything is seen as constantly being, with a sense of total confidence or total pride. There is acknowledgement of everything being, with a sense of self-existing dignity. There is no room to move about or speculate or maneuver. Everything is completely total.

For padma, the total sense of existence also has a tremendous sense of being self-contained. The richness of dignity that has already been developed creates a sense that almost expects or commands magnetism. But again, the terms *command* or *expect* are insufficient or valid only in a relative sense. It is not expecting on the basis of a center-and-fringe notion of this and that; or "command" in the sense of marching into somebody's territory and trying to suck them in. Rather it is like a magnet existing for its own sake rather than having to exercise its magnetic qualities on something else. It is a sort of self-contained magnet.

These five qualities are the basic constituents of the mandala. The reason it is a mandala is because all these qualities relate with each other. It is almost like saying the same thing five different ways. The basic quality of the whole thing is being without a struggle, without a journey. And being without a struggle or journey has different expressions, not because of any relational situation, but just simply as a way of existing. Therefore, we can afford to be free, without aggression, without a fight, without a struggle.

To get into all the meanings of the iconographical details of mandala pictures would require several years of time and space. So trying to put everything into a so-called nutshell, we could say that basic accommodating, or vast being, also contains tremendous power, invincible power, because it does not depend on the existence of the relative world. Since it does not depend on existing in the relative world, it does not need any feedback. Since it does not depend on any feedback, it is not threatened by anything at all. And such 200-percent power (you could almost say, if there is such a thing—we are using relative language again) could be seen as extremely wrathful. This is wrath without anger, without hatred. It is being in a state of invincibility. It is wrath in the sense of a living flame—it does not allow any dualistic or relative concepts to perch on it. If a dualistic situation presented itself, it would be burned up automatically, consumed. But this power contains tremendous peacefulness at the same time. This is not peacefulness in the sense of absence of wrath. That basic space is peaceful because there is no reason that it should not be peaceful, because its totality is always there. Therefore, it is luminous and pure and accommodates everything with nondualistic compassion.

The idea of conflict is generally based on our being trapped in a relative world. The starting point for chaos or confusion is maintaining some point, maintaining some situation. When we try to maintain some point, the occupation that is involved in the process of maintaining is dependent on the threat that comes from all other areas, and that threat channels into the possibility of not being able to maintain. If it were not for that threat, there would be no question of having to maintain at all. The question does not arise at the beginning.

The relationship between maintaining and protecting against the threat to maintaining is like the relationship between zero and one. One is dependent on zero and zero is dependent on one. This is not at all the same as the relationship between one and two. The Sanskrit word *advaya* and the Tibetan word *nyi-me* both express the notion of "not-two," which applies to the relationship between zero and one. In this case it means "no zero, no one." The idea is that as soon as we begin to see in terms of pattern or even begin to imagine or barely think in terms of even vague perceptions of a point of reference, that *is* the birth of both samsara and nirvana (to use the popular terms). The idea of not-two is that it is possible to have a world—a complete, pragmatic world—beyond any point of reference. It is more than possible; it is highly possible. In fact such a world is much more solid than the world of relativity, which is a weak situation based on interdependence, subject to constant death and birth and all kinds of other threats, which constantly arise. With threats constantly arising, the relative situation finally becomes extremely freaky—one never knows who is who, what is what, which is which. It is like the joke "Who's on first, what's on second?"

The dualistic misunderstanding occurs right at the beginning, so when you try to correct it, it just develops into further misunderstandings. But what we are saying is that there is an entirely new area, another dimension, that does not need proof or interpretation. It does not need a reference point. That there is such a dimension is not only highly possible, but it is *so.*

The inspiration of this dimension has developed into beautiful works of art, an imaginary world of nonexistence, a nondualistic world. As personal experience and tradition evolved, 725 basic mandalas were developed, each one of them extremely detailed and precise. One mandala might contain as many as five hundred deities. All those patterns of deities are based on the five principles, the five aspects of the basic space or totality.

This is not just something yogis or siddhas developed by getting drunk on amrita and coming up with things at random.[1] Each point is very definite and very precise. It has been possible to develop a world of precision, a world with a definite clear way of thinking and a functional world, without those other relative areas we have been talking about. It is not only highly possible but it has happened and is happening.

There seem to be a lot of misunderstandings about mandalas. People say that a mandala is an object of meditation that you gaze at. Just by gazing at these colored diagrams you are supposed to get turned on! But from the point of view of sanity, optical illusions or diagrammatic patterns are not crutches you could use to get onto a higher level.

The basic teaching of mandala has been presented 725 times, and that is in the lower tantras, on the level of kriya yoga, alone. Goodness knows how many mandalas there are in the higher tantras—millions of them! The numbers multiply as you go up in the yanas. There are six tantric yanas of which kriya yoga is only the first, and you have 725 mandalas there. As you go up to the level of the sixth yana, ati yoga, the mandalas multiply so many times that they finally become nonexistent. The boundaries begin to dissolve. This is such an invasion of privacy! That is why it is called freedom.

So taking these ideas and attitudes as a functional working basis, we should now be able to provide the conclusion for our seminar.

Visualizing a mandala deity can be approached from two different angles. One way is purely to relate to thought patterns, mind's game. Instead of visualizing Grand Central Station and dwelling on that, you might as well visualize something that means a lot. Eventually, you might visualize the mandala of Avalokiteshvara or Tara or Guhyasamaja or some other deity. That would be a kind of substitute. If you have to have crutches, why not make them out of gold rather than aluminum.

There is another approach to visualization. This is a sense of familiarity with mandala as we have discussed it in this seminar. You turn your attitude toward that sense of mandala with the understanding that you cannot grasp it or nearly grasp it, but such an area does exist. You turn your mind toward it and relate it with your sense of unknown territory and the mysteriousness of the whole of being. That sense of mysteriousness brings all kinds of space. You do not state everything fact by fact. You do not present yourself with a package deal in which everything is logically sound and solid and without any room. You present yourself with some doubt. There is still basic logic, such as that three times three makes nine or whatever, but at the same time you allow some gap, some doubt related to the possibility of a further journey that is necessary. One can turn one's attitude toward that. That is the beginning of the awakening process, a beginning toward giving up your logical game.

Eventually, as we get into the basic mandala as it is, with the whole understanding of samsaric pain and of the dharmadhatu, we realize that the teachings taught in the tradition are not just those of a particular culture. The teachings taught in the language of the tradition are continually up-to-date. Ideally, we should be able to relate to the visualization of a mandala as our own portrait, our own discovery, rather than seeing it as some aspect of a foreign culture that we are dwelling on.

Interestingly, in the Chinese tradition, bodhisattvas, and even certain herukas, or tantric deities, have been depicted wearing Chinese imperial costumes. In India, of course, the place where tantra originated, the deities are depicted as, for instance, Aryan kings, wearing crowns inlaid with the five kinds of jewels along with the rest of the costume of an Aryan king. From this point of view, visualization practice is not entirely anthropomorphic. It is designed or taught for all the six realms of the world: the animal realm, the hell realm, hungry ghost realm, the realm of the jealous gods, realm of the gods, and the human realm.

The tantric approach to practice is absolute, not anthropomorphic. You might say that the hinayana and mahayana
approaches are anthropomorphic, the mahayana approach
somewhat less so. But the vajrayana's approach to practice is
cosmic.[2]

This also goes for the mantras that go along with the
visualizations. They are not regarded as definite words that
make sense—like certain phrases that can keep your mind
from freaking out. Mantra is regarded as the ultimate incan-
tation. There is no room for mind to dwell when what you say
is nonsense—transcendental nonsense. It does not make any
sense, but at the same time it does make sense because of its
nonsense quality. It is just an echo, like the sound of one hand
clapping, a nonexistent sound.

Usually mantra is regarded as an abstract sound rather than
something that means something. In that respect, mantra
recitation is quite different from the usual idea of prayer. It
may be closer to the Hesychastic idea of prayer found in the
Greek Orthodox tradition. The *Philokalia* talks about repeating a prayer over and over. At the beginning you repeat it
with intention, with direction, with a sense of purpose. You
go on and on and on. Finally, you are uncertain who is saying
the prayer and who is not saying it. You lose the sense of
direction. You actually become free of the sense of direction
rather than losing it in the sense of getting confused. You
become less confused, therefore you become more accommodating. Eventually, the prayer begins to repeat as though it
were the beat of your heart, as though it were repeating itself.
In fact at that point, the prayer is repeating you rather than
you are repeating the prayer. This kind of prayer has some
connection with the mantric approach.

The mantric approach starts at the beginning, not even as a
prayer but just as a certain cosmic sound that goes along with
a certain cosmic visualization. The visualization might be of

mandalas or various deities, maybe a six-armed deity with eighteen heads, holding different sceptres in its hands, wearing a human skin with an elephant skin on top of it, wearing a tiger skin as a skirt and a crown of skulls, surrounded by flame, and uttering magic words such as HUM and PHAT. Such visualizations are very vivid. However, they are by no means pop art. They are transcendental art. These expressions become extraordinarily powerful and vivid and real to the extent that we are able to give up the boundaries of the dualistic approach of evaluating them. Once there is no more evaluation, the whole thing becomes very lively, very real.

The problem that arises for us in relation to this is that first we have to have a definite sense of commitment to ourselves. We have to be willing to work with the samsaric mandala to begin with, without looking for something better. We have to make the best of samsaric situations and work with them. After we have worked with samsaric situations, we gradually develop an awareness of the background, or environment, in which the samsaric mandala functions. We begin to discover that there is something more than just this world alone, than the world in our dualistic sense of it.

I do not mean to say that there is another world somewhere else, like the moon, Mars, or the heavens. There is another world in the sense that there is another discovery that we could make. We see a blade of grass, but we could see further into its blade of grassness. We could see the blade of grass in its own full totality. Then we would see the greenness of the blade of grass as part of its innate nature. Its whole being is actually being, without any confirmation. It just happens to be a really true blade of grass. When the mandala experience begins to occur, we see the true world, 100 percent, without distortion, without conceptualizing it.

It takes a lot of steps, and it seems that we cannot begin unless we are willing to begin at the beginning.

STUDENT: Apropos of the beginning, you said the dualistic misunderstanding comes right at the beginning. Does a glimpse or taste of the nondualistic totality also come at the beginning?

TRUNGPA RINPOCHE: Yes. That is why a misunderstanding was possible. The misunderstanding had to be accommodated somewhere. So we can't condemn the beginning as a mistake in the fashion of the "Fall of Man."

STUDENT: In the question period following the previous talk, you seemed to be speaking of a sense of greater spaciousness in connection with prajna. You connected nonduality more with jnana. I don't really understand this.

TRUNGPA RINPOCHE: Prajna is like what we experience in connection with our discussions in this and the other talks. We talk about jnana and the level of absolute totality, but in so doing we are relating to it from an outsider's point of view, we are relating to it as an experience. That way it becomes prajna, or knowledge—information. It is prajna until we completely and totally identify with the whole thing. The process of being is not learning how to be. Learning and just being are different.

S: Your discussion of vajra suggests that it operates on the prajna level, that it is subject-and-object oriented. Is that correct?

TR: The vajra experience of intellect is on the jnana level. It is just totally seeing through everything. That transcends prajna, which is still somewhat of an adolescent approach.

S: On the nondualistic level, can there be such things as buddha families and prajna and the world of distinctions?

TR: That is exactly what we have been saying is the case in this talk. The level of nondual reality is the realm of jnana, therefore there is discriminating-awareness wisdom happening all the time. On that level, there is in fact a living world, a much more living one than we are experiencing.

S: It sounds like there would be a contradiction there, because to discriminate is to find duality.

TR: There is no problem with finding duality. We are speaking here of the relative world in purely psychological terms. We are talking about relative fixation, relative hang-ups, rather than seeing things as two. That is not regarded as dualistic fixation but still as discriminating awareness. I mean, an enlightened person is able to go down the street and take his bus—as a matter of fact, he can do it much better than we can, because he is always there.

STUDENT: In terms of beginning at the beginning, what is the role of meditation practice?

TRUNGPA RINPOCHE: Meditation practice right at the beginning is acceptance of being a fool. You continually acknowledge that you are making a fool out of yourself pretending to be meditating, rather than believing you are transcending something or being holy or good. If you start from that matter-of-fact level, acknowledging your self-deceptions, then you begin to pick up on something more than being a fool. There's something in it. You begin to learn to give. You no longer have to defend yourself constantly. So that practice involves tremendous discipline in your daily living situation. It is not just sitting practice alone, but your total life situation becomes part of your meditation practice. That provides a lot of ground for relating with things very simply, without concepts involved. And then at some stage, of course, you begin to lose any sense of effort or self-conscious awareness that you are meditating. The boundaries of your meditation begin to dissolve, and it becomes nonmeditation or all meditation.

S: Isn't that initial wanting also spiritual materialism?

TR: It is, but at least it is quite genuine rather than pretended. That makes things simpler. Obviously, at the beginning you feel you want to achieve something. That is okay, and it helps you get into the practice. In the case of spiritual materialism, the deceptive aspect is that you do not even face the facts of your neurosis. Each time you practice something, you think in terms of getting some magical power, trying to become powerful instead of unmasking yourself. But without that initial wanting there would be no stepping-stone, no language. Seeing that situation is exactly what I mean by regarding yourself as a fool.

STUDENT: Rinpoche, could you please explain again what you mean by accommodating?

TRUNGPA RINPOCHE: It is a sense of nondefensiveness, accommodating richness or expansiveness and the magnetic qualities without making a solid boundary. It is not an effort; it is just letting things be accommodated without any relative relationship.

STUDENT: How does this highly intellectual talk get us closer to nirvana and farther from samsara?

TRUNGPA RINPOCHE: If you approach it from that angle, it doesn't.

S: Of course not, but isn't that the angle from which it is being approached?

TR: We always have to speak in relative language, which automatically becomes intellectual.

S: Granted the need to speak in relative language, I have still found this talk quite confusing.

TR: That seems to be the whole point. We should realize that there is some discrepancy, that everything is not clear-cut and black and white. Feeling confused is the starting point. When you are confused, you don't believe in your confusion as being the answer. Because you are confused, you feel that the answer must be something else more clear. That invites further questioning, which contains the answer within itself. One begins to work on oneself that way.

In other words, the teaching is not meant to provide something sound and solid and precise, in such a way that you don't have to work for anything and the teaching feeds you constantly. The reason for presenting the teaching is to make you work further, to confuse you more. And you have to get through the confusion. The teaching is encouragement to find the stepping-stone that is closest to you—which is confusion.

STUDENT: Would you say that unconditioned, nondualistic energies have as resources the energies that are still conditioned?

TRUNGPA RINPOCHE: I wouldn't say that. The unconditioned energies are self-perpetuating, because there are no relations involved. They exist like space itself, which does not have a central point or an edge. It remains as it is by itself, feeds itself, lives by itself. The conditioned energies are also accommodated within this unconditioned one. Somehow the unconditioned energy can express itself in terms of the conditioned ones. But it doesn't survive or feed on them. That's why conditioned energy is redundant from the point of view of unconditioned energy. It doesn't need to exist. That is why it stagnates. There is no outlet for it, and it becomes a self-perpetuating dying and rotting process. The only way it can maintain itself is to get energy from itself, and it is already very stagnant.

STUDENT: You mentioned that the Chinese developed different visualizations for the various deities and pointed out that the tradition is always up to date. I was wondering if we American Buddhists might develop our own visualizations of the deities that might be more appropriate for us.

S: For example, mahakalas in blue jeans.[3]

TRUNGPA RINPOCHE: Fat chance!

In China, the process was very unself-conscious. It just evolved that way. But in the West, we are in a highly self-conscious state about culture—it has already been raped. All of art has already been raped and made into a conditioned situation. The tradition would get made into pop art or collage—having a Tibetan painting with an astronaut walking across it or something of that nature. The situation with regard to art has become quite degenerate.

The point is that if we could make the process less self-conscious, something could develop, but since we already have a self-conscious world, that would probably be very difficult. In fact, the same problem existed in Tibet. The Chinese took the whole thing very freely, but the Tibetans were very self-conscious about their culture. They regarded it as inferior to the Aryan culture of India. The Indians used to refer to Tibet as the *preta-puri*, the place of hungry ghosts. They regarded it as uncultured and savage. So the Tibetans became very self-conscious about it. Therefore, instead of creating Tibetan deities, they decided to take refuge in the Aryan culture from the beginning. So in Tibet there are no Tibetans in the form of Vairochana or anything like that. That is an interesting analogy.

STUDENT: When an offering is made in the form of a mandala, what is that and how is it done? For example, Naropa is described as offering Tilopa a mandala.

TRUNGPA RINPOCHE: Well, that is not a mandala in the sense of a psychological or spiritual one. It's just a portrait of the world with the continents and oceans and everything. Making that offering represents giving up your ground so that you have nowhere to live. That is the ultimate sense of "refugee."

STUDENT: Is there such a thing as a pure expression of pure energy?

TRUNGPA RINPOCHE: It would mean getting out of the whirlpool of the relative world. Then it would become open for the very reason that it would no longer be dependent on the relative world.

STUDENT: From the point of view of "not-two," how does compassion arise?

TRUNGPA RINPOCHE: Just not dwelling on a point of reference provides a lot of space to be. Compassion is open space in which things can be accommodated. It contrasts strongly with our repulsing situations because we are not willing to accommodate anything. So compassion is creating open space, accepting things happening.

S: How do you create that openness?

TR: If you have to create it, then it is no longer compassion. I suppose, to begin with, in order to develop compassion you have to be willing to be alone or lonely. You are completely and totally in a desolate situation, which is also open space at the same time. The development of compassion is not a matter of acquiring a partnership with things, but rather of letting everything be open. So the sense of loneliness or aloneness is the real starting point for compassion.

STUDENT: In the beginning of the seminar, you talked a lot about boundary, and now you have talked about the mandala as being boundless. Can you clarify that?

TRUNGPA RINPOCHE: The samsaric mandala is divided by

boundaries, because there are certain emotions and psychological states; they are there because you maintain them to survive. The total mandala, the mandala of totality, is not dependent on boundaries at all. Therefore, its expressions are regarded as different aspects of one totality. The accommodating aspect of space and the penetrating [or expansive] aspect of space are simply different aspects of the same thing. You could talk about the light-giving aspect of the sun and the fertility-producing aspect of the sun, or the sun as the basis for timing our lives—that is all talking about different aspects of the same thing. There are no boundaries there, just different expressions.

S: Should the boundaries be considered as a real principle of reality or existence?

TR: Boundaries happen like taking a snapshot. You take a snapshot, say, at 1/125th of a second. You take the snapshot, and it is frozen on a piece of paper.

STUDENT: What is the relationship between what you talked about earlier, experiencing the charnel ground through a sense of insecurity, and seeing the totality, which seems to be the key to the buddha mandala?

TRUNGPA RINPOCHE: Totality shares the attributes of insecurity. When the samsaric mind views totality, it sees insecurity, a threat, a place to die. Totality is extremely threatening because there is nothing to hold onto. It is completely vast space. Whereas from its own point of view, totality does not contain any kind of reference point. Therefore, the question of threat or insecurity does not arise at all.

We have to stop at this point. It would be good to work further on the things we discussed, reflect on them and relate them with your experience. What we have talked about is the meaning of space, which is something that, in our everyday life, we all automatically face. In the city or on the farm, in our family situation or at our job, we are constantly involved with space. So the relationship with the mandala goes on—at least the irritating aspect. It is not something we can turn off, thinking, "Now I've gotten my money's worth, I'll just switch it off and forget it." No matter how much we try to forget it, it continues to go on. So it is not merely a matter of having acquired some information; there is some element of commitment, because the totality of your life is involved. We have to relate with our life situations and find out more.

TWO

Mandala of the Five Buddha Families

KARME-CHÖLING 1974

The Basic Ground

In order to understand the mandala of the five buddha families, I think it is necessary for us to realize the implications of the mandala principle in terms of our psychological state and our awareness in our everyday lives.

First of all, there are some points concerning the ground that is in some sense serving our being. That is the ground of the five buddha families. The five buddha-family principles are not five separate entities. Rather, what we have is one principle manifested in five different aspects. We could speak of five different manifestations of one basic energy: a manifestation of its richness, of its fertility, of its intelligence, and so forth.

We are talking about one basic intelligence, so to speak, or one energy. A wide area of confusion and wisdom exists in the background of all the five principles, whether we look at them in their buddha, or enlightened, form or in their confused form. There is a basic pattern that is common to all that. It is the potentiality for enlightenment and the actual experience of confusion, pain, and so forth.

We are experiencing our existence, our being. If you look further into what that is, intellectually you can analyze it in all kinds of different ways. But if you are trying to find out what it is all about in terms of actual experience, it is hard to find the actual experience. It is hard, very hard, to find even a clear experience of confusion, one that is not colored by the rest of the emotions. In the actual experience, there is also a sense of uncertainty concerning existence or nonexistence (both being the same thing). It is not that we have a vague perception. It is a very clear perception, but it is undefinably clear. It is basically confusion. That kind of confusion is all-pervasive confusion; it happens throughout our life, in our waking hours and during our sleep. There is a rich and thick bank of uncertainty.

If we get into religious or metaphysical terminology, we could call it a soul or ego or godhead, or any number of other things. But if we do not want to use those kinds of terms because we do not know exactly what they mean, then we have to try to look as directly as possible at this experience without any preconceptions, without any terminology or labels. If we look closely, the closest experience we can get is a sense of unnameable confusion. This is a unique confusion, because it does not have a clear and distinct quality of "now I am confused" at all. You cannot even define it by saying it is confusion. And that is the kind of nondual state of confusion that goes on throughout all life.

Experience comes out of that and dissipates back into it. Energies arise and emotions appear. It all takes place within this one all-pervasive state of being, or area. I think it is very important for us to realize this background as the basic ground of everything and to understand how it arises or does not arise.

In traditional tantric imagery, this experience, or state of being, is referred to as the charnel ground. It is the place of birth and the place of death. It is the place you came out of and the place you return to. The modern equivalent of that, I suppose, is the hospital—the place where you are born and die.

Anyhow, this gigantic hospital is quite messy, but unnameably messy and nondual—that is the one point. Usually, when we think of there being no duality, no split, no schizophrenia, we tend to think that this is some kind of meditative state where there are no longer any dualistic distinctions. Therefore, everything must be okay. But somehow things don't work that way here. Actually, we seem to have nondual samsara at this point. This is quite interesting.

Obviously, following logic, if you have duality or a split personality, there must be something in the background that was one thing to begin with. Out of that one comes many. One of the interesting things here is that somehow that basic confusion acts as a continual sense of awareness. This goes beyond purely human consciousness. It covers animals and humans and all the rest of existence.

Somehow, though it is a confused state, it does not seem to contain any doubt as such. As soon as you begin to have doubt, then there is a play back and forth. But this state is pervasive, so there is no room for this kind of play of doubt. Maybe this is the background for doubt, but there is no doubt as such. It seems to be a big, gigantic state of BLAH. People have misunderstood this as a mystical experience.

Perhaps in some sense it actually is a mystical experience, because unless you have some glimpse of this level of basic ignorance, you cannot have a glimpse of the rest. From this point of view, maybe finding the worst aspect of oneself is the first glimpse of the possibility of being better.

This is the basic ground of the mandala of the five buddha principles in both their samsaric and their nirvanic aspects. Both aspects have a common relationship with this background.

Well, we could talk a lot more about this basic ground, but

I do not want to create any further sense of glamour regarding it. We already have some idea of it, and it would be very good if you had a chance to look into it further yourself.

STUDENT: Is this confusion the cloudy mind of the seventh consciousness?[1]

TRUNGPA RINPOCHE: It goes back further than that.

S: But does it manifest in the cloudy mind as well?

TR: This is the alaya level, which goes back further than the seventh consciousness. It has some kind of texture of being, of existence. It is not cloudy in the sense of an obstruction of vision or intelligence. That would be more on the perception level. In this case, it is more sort of basically clogged up, rather than there being something that is projected and then clouded over. This is more on an existential level. That is why it can be so transparent and act as a constant awareness of ego, of me. You have a feeling of "me." Before you mention me, there is a sense of this direction. Before you actually define it as a reference to me, there is a sense of direction toward this area and a sense of heaviness and solidity.

S: You mean a holding back? One is always holding back or pushing something?

TR: No, I mean even before that. This is a kind of self-existing awareness that contains an automatic reference to you already, so you don't have to hold back or project. Before you do anything, there is the first instant that makes you start from here, rather than from all over the place. Then you have a starting point somewhere.

S: Is this something that is carried with you from one life to another?

TR: I suppose so, because belief in life is in itself a grasping of being. Yes. Otherwise, the continuity of life's thread is broken.

S: I have heard something about ego being continuous over many lives. Would this be a sense of that? It is somehow nondualistic but it is still a tendency to identify "me"?

TR: Yes. There is that chain reaction that is basically a broken chain reaction, but it is still obviously a chain, because one link constantly interlinks with another one.

S: Is this confusion something that we are aware of in our own lives personally, and is it also connected at the same time with some kind of more primordial confusion that we pass through each time we come into another life?

TR: I think we are aware of it, not as something clearly defined in terms of concepts and ideas, but as you said, it is primordial. It is the first cause of reactions. It is the first activator, or the first ground that activation could come from.

S: And this activation brings us into this form that we call body and mind?

TR: Yes. There is a sense of this and that to begin with, and of me and mine.

STUDENT: I'm a little unclear about the seventh and eighth consciousnesses and the level of duality here. It seems that what you're talking about must be a relative nonduality in comparison to, say, the nondual unconditioned energy of the dharmakaya. What you're talking about seems to be based on some kind of an ego notion or an ego-based perception. How can this be nondual? Is there some kind of relative nonduality here?

TRUNGPA RINPOCHE: The reference point exists for the sake of the reference point, I suppose. As far as this particular state is concerned, it is seemingly nondual, because the definition of duality is based on perceiving "that" because of "this." But this level of ignorance does not have the facilities to separate, to make this distinction. This is not because it is so highly unified with all the energies, as with the dharmakaya or enlightened nonduality, but because it has not developed to that extent. This is primitive nonduality. It is sort of primordial, or rather primeval—like an amoeba or something like that. But it does have a very low level of intelligence, therefore it has awareness in it as well. It is on the level of a grain of sand.

S: So this level of consciousness can never recognize itself? It has no self-consciousness?

TR: That's right, it doesn't have self-consciousness, but it has a sense of trust in oneself. It is sort of homey, you know; it's easy to operate on that basis, on the basis of that homey quality. If you are in doubt, you just blank yourself, then you proceed. It is very convenient in some sense.

S: Are you suggesting that some kind of manipulation is possible with this? That when you're in doubt, you just blank yourself?

TR: Well, that's not exactly manipulation; it's just the best that you can do. If you feel uncertain, you go back to the source. That is what we usually do, you know. If you lose a job somewhere else, you come back to your home town; you stay with your mommy and daddy for a while.

S: In books, you often read about mystical experiences that people have had where they say there was nobody there, no me, just a big void. Do you think they could be experiencing this basic confusion you're talking about here?

TR: It depends how far people reach. I think it is possible that they just manage to hit this level and do not get beyond it. This is like what is said in relation to tantric practice, about doing visualization without having had a glimpse of shunyata. It just leads to ego. It depends on your level of fundamental clarity and luminosity. You might experience a state of nonfunctionality, nonduality, maybe even void, but without any light. That doesn't say very much. It's like a deep coma.

S: That would be where your clarity has broken down?

TR: If there's no clarity, things would be purely in a state of stupidity. It seems that the voidness, or emptiness, of shunyata occurs automatically if there's some sense of clarity. But it seems that there is some clarity there at the same time, and this is the seed for the five buddha principles, or the reason why the five buddha principles do exist. Those principles are a statement of clarity in the different areas. You have clarity that is vajralike, clarity that is ratnalike, padmalike, karmalike, and buddhalike. All the energies are a state of clarity and luminosity.

S: So you can't skip the stages of developing clarity and just jump to a clear experience of shunyata?

TR: That's possible, but I don't think it is very healthy. You could be overwhelmed by such brilliance; it would just make you more blind. It would be like having someone switch on the sun at midnight.

S: Is there a normal, effective way to discover what that light is?

TR: Light?

S: The clarity.

TR: There obviously has to be something, otherwise there would be no relationship between the two worlds [of confusion and enlightenment], so to speak. The only way seems to be breaking through the levels of comfort that your stupidity feels. You know, when you are on a level of this kind of stupidity, there is a sense of comfort, a sense of indulgence. So I suppose the first step is becoming homeless, so that you have nowhere to go back to.

S: Does this mean that reaching a certain degree of despair is essential?

TR: I think so, yes. That has been said.

S: Would this despair mean feeling that there's no way out of your neurosis, or does it come from feeling that there *is* a way to work with it?

TR: You do feel possibilities of working with it, but not of shaking off the whole thing completely. Then there is also despair arising from a sense of temporary inconvenience—you can't return back to your cozy stupid home.

STUDENT: With this nondual confusion being so diffuse, is there any particular reason why there are just five buddha families? Is it possible there might be another one? Why have five buddha families arisen out of this ground of confusion? Is there any particular meaning to that?

TRUNGPA RINPOCHE: There's no particular meaning to that. It just organically happened that way. Somehow everything breaks into four sections, along with the middle section. For instance, we have four directions. Of course, you can invent numerous directions, but even if you have a hundred directions, they are still based on the logic of the four directions. That's just how things work. There is perception and there is appreciation of that.

In the tantric texts we sometimes find references to 100 families and sometimes there are even 999 families. But these are exaggerated forms of the five principles. There don't have to be five, particularly, but that's as close as you can get. It's sort of like a baker's dozen.

STUDENT: I didn't quite follow how this basic awareness functions as a home.

TRUNGPA RINPOCHE: It's the closest thing we can come back to. It's like reducing ourselves to being deaf and dumb— you don't have to pay attention to too many things. You just simplify everything into one livable situation. That's the concept of hominess—you can shut off the rest of the world, shut out the world outside. You can come back and have dinner and a good sleep. It's a primitive kind of thing, like a nest.

S: So being out there—

TR: Is more demanding.

S: Is what you're speaking of prepersonal though? If I think of myself as having a meal and going to sleep, it feels very personal. I'm home, and that's very personal; it's me doing it. Is that what you're talking about, or is it before that?

TR: That's right, before that, prior to that.

STUDENT: I have an image sometimes of being inside a rock, which would clearly be pre-this. It's that kind of state.

TRUNGPA RINPOCHE: That's right, yes. It's vague in some sense, it's unnameable. It doesn't have any kind of manifest expressions.

S: I have a sense of despair or pain that comes from the realization that I can't go back to that level of stupidity again. It's like I'm stuck at this mediocre stage. Does that have something to do with the despair you were talking about, that one can't return?

TR: In some sense. Different people would have different reactions. Some people would like to go back, because it is much easier. They have done it before; it is pre-rehearsed. Other people feel that it is too much to do it all over again. It depends on the level of one's intelligence and how much one has already gone sour on it.

STUDENT: You're speaking of this basic background as a samsaric approach of some kind. Is that the case?

TRUNGPA RINPOCHE: It is a sort of feeling of me, this [places his hand on his chest] direction, a kind of primordial ego. If we speak of threefold ignorance, this is the first one, the ignorance of being. This relates to the basic state of being, primordial existence. In some sense this is a very refined version of samsara; in some sense it is a very crude one. The reason it is categorized as samsaric is that it is based on the preservation of oneself. Whether it is a refined job or a crude job, it still has to do with the preservation of one's existence. It is pro-ego, definitely. It may be unconsciously so, but it is still pro-ego. It is connected with building something up rather than letting go. Still, in terms of the path, it is a necessary stepping-stone, a working basis.

2

The Birth of the Path

In continuing our discussion of the fundamentals of ego experience, I would like to make clear to you that what we are saying here is based on personal experience. We are taking more of an intuitive approach than an intellectual one.

A lot of energy comes along with the primitive ignorance. The basic function of that ignorance is a sense of boredom and familiarity, and that produces a desire for some further excitement, further adventure. That adventure becomes somewhat neurotic, because of our not having surveyed the ground and ourselves. This is the point where duality begins to happen.

At the beginning, duality is just a way of killing boredom; then there is the realization that taking this kind of chance is very dangerous. As we continue on, things become more threatening. We begin to develop various perspectives, various tones of emphasis on various types of styles. At this point, what are known as the five buddha families manifest in five confused styles: an aggressive, intellectual one; an enriching one; a seductive, magnetizing one; a highly active one; and so on. The expressions that tend to come out at this point are ones that have some quality of desperation in relation to the basic ground. The desperation is based on [and takes the form of] the style that one is able to operate in, in order to ignore the basic ignorance.

In other words, all the things that happen in confused mind are fundamentally a way of overcoming boredom and entertaining oneself, on one hand, and a way of taking one's mind off threats, on the other. The main threat is that if one happened to return to the background, one might see the sense of embarrassing confusion that exists there and the struggle to conceal one's private parts.

There are various levels of ignorance. The first level of ignorance is connected with having a body. One's style of life is affected by what kind of body one has. One's behavior pattern is molded to one's body. There is a natural body consciousness that takes place. You may be big or small, fat or thin; whatever your bodily makeup is like, you create a way of organizing a smooth operation of behavior in accordance with that. That kind of natural self-consciousness takes place all the time. If you are cold, you never think, "My body is cold," but rather, "I am cold," "I am hungry," and so forth. There is a natural tendency to identify one's body with one's state of existence, or being.

So that kind of basic ignorance is constantly there, and whenever there is an area that is uncertain, a slight gap, or something unexpected—if something does not go along with the program one has set up for one's own behavior—then an element of panic and uncertainty arises which then pushes one to take certain actions. These actions are connected with the five styles. We are not talking about which of the five styles might be our personal style, but about a general, almost haphazard or random type of improvisation that takes place constantly in our lives—trying to fill the gap and trying to entertain.

How does this experience of the five buddha principles relate with the path of buddhadharma? Somehow, within that sense of lost ground, within that continual self-consciousness, there is also at the same time a sense of intelligence. This intelligence actually does not come from anywhere, it does not have an origin. Or perhaps at this point we should say we are uncertain where it comes from. In any case, there is this intelligence that tends to comment on the things that take place. It begins to see the functions of the self-conscious, basic, primordial ego. It sees the basic ego as it is, and it also sees the various trips, so to speak, that we get into to safeguard ourselves from boredom or whatever. So there is this constant commenting that takes place, which is the beginning of the path.

This intelligence is an inborn intelligence of some kind, one that is without origin or birth as such. It is usually awakened with the help of a teacher or by seeing someone else's example, their approach to life and their wisdom. It is not a simple case of the teacher's giving birth to that intelligence in one's being. It is impossible for such a direct transplant to take place, since the intelligence is already part of our being. But quite certainly, this intelligence can be awakened.

The process of awakening that intelligence is basically one of sabotage or of instigating an uprising. It sets chaos into the well-settled programs and policies that develop within ego's space. The intelligence often works with emotions and also often works along with ego's tendencies, so it is somewhat transparent [as far as taking sides is concerned]. It does not always act as the saboteur; sometimes it just works as a kind of hired workman who complains heavily to his employer but at the same time goes along with him. It works in both areas. It works with ego, which uses intelligence, but at the same time there is an undercurrent or a kind of percolation happening. This is the birth of the path taking place.

This process exaggerates the neurosis of the five principles further, because a very threatening situation is developing. Things are getting very personal and much, much closer to the heart.

STUDENT: Are the styles that arise determined karmically—is there a certain sketch that exists in you that you automatically fulfill? Or is there some spontaneous process of intelligence involved?

TRUNGPA RINPOCHE: The process is natural and extremely organic. There are no particular guidelines. Awareness just approaches the closest thing that is available and does it. But there is obviously some kind of style that is connected with the habitual patterns of the elements—water flows, fire burns, that kind of natural thing. There is no intelligence operating at that level except the partial intelligence that is trying to avoid seeing the original background. That seems to be the only logical or intelligent function that is happening. The rest of it is very sort of animal-level.

STUDENT: If the neurotic styles are based on one's body type, what would the five enlightened styles be based on?

TRUNGPA RINPOCHE: Well, that is just an analogy. I suppose one does [base one's behavior pattern on one's body], but I don't think that has anything to do with one's particular neurosis or reality. That's just a way of functioning—if you have a body, you have to behave in a certain way. But there are no particular guidelines.

STUDENT: Is there any reason that one person would fall into one style rather than another? Is there something in one's personal makeup?

TRUNGPA RINPOCHE: I think it is a question of the different forms of irritation that come up in relating with the background of ego, irritations connected with how you want to go about covering up or ignoring. There are a lot of aspects of that which can be dealt with in different ways.

S: Would this carry over from one lifetime to another?

TR: Not necessarily. It is simply a day-to-day kind of thing.

STUDENT: It seems that we are working through the eight levels of consciousness.[1] We talked earlier about the alaya, and then you started talking about the basic notion of duality coming into the *nyön yi* [the seventh consciousness]. How does this apply to the other states of consciousness? As we extend into the other six consciousnesses, does that simply further the confusion?

TRUNGPA RINPOCHE: Theoretically, what we are talking about here happens at the level of the sixth consciousness, which is mind, the mental faculty, which then relates with the sense perceptions. But I think this could also cover a lot of areas other than consciousness, for instance, feeling, perception, impulse—those other skandhas.[2] This is a very early stage; nothing is really properly fixed. This is just the level of groping around and trying to develop a system. No rules and regulations or styles have been developed; there is just a groping. It's the level of feeling, the second skandha.

STUDENT: When you were talking about how these styles are motivated, you said that one aspect of the motive was avoiding boredom. Then you mentioned avoiding the threat that one might fade into the background. I am confused. You mentioned those two things, and I don't see how they fit together.

TRUNGPA RINPOCHE: In fact, there seem to be [not just those two, but] a lot of motivations. Those are just random choices. There are hundreds of other possibilities connected with all kinds of areas of irritation and uncertainty. There are hundreds of areas of irritation and uncertainty—lots of them. And then there is just roaming around in animal stupidity and having things just happen to coincide with one situation or another, which is another type of approach. Traditionally, motivation here is divided into three sections connected with passion, aggression, and ignorance. But within that framework, there are lots of descriptions. Supposedly, there are 84,000 variations.

STUDENT: You seemed to talk about a blockage in connection with ignorance and confusion. Is this a blockage that prevents us from exploring the whole question of whether we exist or not, the whole question of existence and nonexistence?

TRUNGPA RINPOCHE: Somehow the whole idea of existence and nonexistence never came up. But there is the possibility of its coming up. Once that idea has been heard, then there is the possibility of nonexistence—of intelligence looking back at oneself and finding and cutting through various trips. Until the idea of nonexistence has been heard, this possibility never comes up. So hearing the teachings can be very shocking. Until the teachings have been heard, things are seemingly smooth. There is a sort of gentleman's agreement that one never talks about those things, or in this case, even thinks about them.

STUDENT: Was Naropa's jumping off roofs and going into sandalwood fires symbolic of his exploring this whole question of existence and nonexistence and somehow breaking through the blockages?

TRUNGPA RINPOCHE: I think we find all kinds of connections in his life with that. He marries the king's daughter and then the kingdom disappears, and all kinds of other things of that nature happen. All those things are very much connected with that. There is a reality of some kind, but it is a very painful reality. Then, after you have experienced the painful reality and feel that you have done a good job in relating with it, then somehow you realize the whole thing doesn't exist. This is also very painful, because you thought that at least you had achieved something. You thought you had broken the ice, and then suddenly no ice exists to be broken. That is the kind of thing that makes up the nature of the path.

STUDENT: Does the fact that there are 84,000 styles mean that it is not possible to go through the human condition in a way that is not conditioned by one of them? Or is there another kind of humanity that is free of that?

TRUNGPA RINPOCHE: It is not limited to 84,000, but there are hundreds of thousands of them. In other words, you cannot have a complete manual of what the human condition might be. You cannot follow all the details; you can only look at an aerial view of the situation. You can see where those styles are derived from and where they are heading (which would be the same thing). It's like the analogy of all rivers flowing into the ocean. You can predict that much, even though you can't name all the rivers in the world. There are some overall conclusions that you can draw. In this case, the basic point is trying to exist, trying to live through one's life without being hurt, hurt in any way, even slightly hurt; trying just to have complete freedom and pleasure. And in some sense the teachings represent the opposite of that. They say that that is not particularly the way. Not only can you not achieve survival, you cannot actually exist, let alone survive. Survival is the opposite [of the right approach]. You know, you have the wrong end of the stick. So then we are back to square one.

STUDENT: I thought the previous question was whether it was possible to avoid those styles and just have an open experience of humanity without being conditioned by them.

TRUNGPA RINPOCHE: Those styles are the contents. It isn't possible, I can't imagine it.

S: How does the multiplicity and variety of the styles come out of that one basic energy?

TR: If there is one basic energy or one basic approach, that does not have to produce another *one,* but it could produce many. If you have one big bad weather, there are hundreds of raindrops. It is possible, it is conceivable, and it happens. It like the blind men's version of the elephant—you have different versions. From the very fact that everybody agrees together that they are blind comes a lot of other conclusions.

S: It seems there would have to be some duality or something for this oneness to be affected by.

TR: It happens as you come out of the oneness, I suppose. When you are on your way out, you break up into different reflections.

S: But what is breaking you?

TR: What's breaking you is that there is more room to play about. When you are not restricted by the oneness, there is a sense of breaking off from it—or a better expression would be, indulging in the freedom—in different ways. You find different ways of indulging in freedom. If you come from the same home as your six brothers and seven sisters, when each one of you steps beyond the restrictions of your parents' rule, you will establish different lifestyles, just because of no longer being restricted by your parents' command. The break takes place because you want proof that you exist. And the different styles arise from that.

S: But if the basic background is the same for everybody, how do the different styles come to be different?

TR: Because the basic background is the same, therefore

there can be differences. Otherwise, if the basic background were different, then the expressions would be the same. That's worth thinking about actually. The basic background is one, not exactly one in the sense of one entity, but one in the sense of being all-pervasive, filling everywhere. Then something happens out of that that allows us to step out. And as we step out, there are possibilities of moving about in that big room. Those possibilities come just from the very fact that that area is a big one, an all-encompassing one.

S: So it's an interaction between you and the space.

TR: It is like having a big floor—you finally begin to dance, to move about. You move because there is oneness of you and the space. The oneness allows you to move more. It gives you some kind of freedom. In this case, that freedom is somewhat distorted, but nevertheless the process is one of looking for freedom of some kind, or demonstrating one's freedom.

STUDENT: Is there some kind of predetermined relationship between a particular style of ignorance and intelligence as represented in the mandala and the form that it takes on the human level? Is it all predetermined before it takes human form, or is it something more socialized, something that develops as one grows up living with one's six brothers and seven sisters and then goes out into the world?

TRUNGPA RINPOCHE: That is very hard to answer. I think it is more of an accident in some sense, somewhat a matter of chance. But there is some kind of determining factor that tends to create that chance itself. So, if I may say so, it's both; it has both elements in it at the same time. It is not so well defined. You are prone to a lot of accidents. And the more your intelligence develops and the more prepared for the teachings you become, the more you are prone to accidents. Somehow these accidents come out of some kind of intelligence that is based on the weakening of the basic strategy. The basic strategy begins to fall apart slightly, so there are less defense mechanisms taking place. Therefore, you are prone to more accidents.

STUDENT: You talked about there being the basic all-pervasive oneness, and then all of a sudden there is a duality situation of some kind, which I understood as the first skandha. What I don't understand is that you said the reason one can move about is that one is one with the space. It's a situation of being one and not being one at the same time, which seems quite paradoxical.

TRUNGPA RINPOCHE: I think that is the case.

Well, we could intellectualize the whole thing and turn it into madhyamaka logic. But we should try as much as possible not to do that. Using an experiential approach at this point is more efficacious. So, [experientially speaking, the point is] that in order to accomplish an experience, you have to have a chance to dance with it. You have to have a chance to play, to explore. And then each style of exploration that takes place, we could say, is a different manifestation. Nevertheless it is all part of one big game. It's all the same thing. This is like the traditional analogy that says the beads of a mala [a rosary] are one, not a hundred, because if there are a hundred pieces, you can't have one mala.

S: Is there something about the totality of the ignorance, the totality of the way the ignorance covers the ground, that is the same as the way each one of these primordial energies also covers the ground? Experientially, I mean.

TR: Yes. Otherwise, you couldn't function. I mean, you do have some driving force behind you.

S: So there is a certain way that intelligence is relating with the totality of the ignorance?

TR: Yes. That is why the intelligence, that is, the message of the teachings, becomes more threatening: there is no room left for escape. The whole area is completely covered.

S: Can your basic energy change in the course of your life, say, as you move from childhood to adulthood?

TR: I suppose you can change your opinion about things, but the basic energy remains the same. Moving from childhood to adulthood is not particularly a big deal. It's just a question of becoming professional. It's like learning to open a wine bottle with a corkscrew. The first time, you may spill the wine all over; the second and the third time you get better; by the fifth time you are good at it. That development has nothing to do with the basic energy particularly. It's just improving your mind-body coordination.

STUDENT: You spoke of trying to fill the gap. Is the gap the same for all people?

TRUNGPA RINPOCHE: It is not so much a question of whether the gap is the same gap, but how the boundary is, whether the boundary is fat or thin. The gap is always the same. The gap depends on the boundary, I suppose.

S: I don't understand. Is the gap boredom, or what is it?

TR: Anything. The gap is something that you cannot utilize as part of your energy. It is something slightly foreign, but it is still part of you. It could be boredom, uncertainty, ignorance—any gap, any absence of ego, for that matter (which comes later, I suppose).

S: Is this a sense of panic that is a form of intelligence? Is this a manifestation of intelligence we are talking about?

TR: It depends what happens after you panic. There is a sense of intelligence in the panic. If, after you have panicked, you do not resort again to more entertainment, if you let yourself be suspended a little bit, then that panic is much closer to reality, more dharmic, if I may use that word.

S: More precisely aware of what is going on?

TR: Yes. The other panic is just, you know, diving into more deep water.

S: How do you let yourself be suspended? What is the process of going that way rather than diving?

TR: Well, in our discussion, we are trying to work with personal experience rather than developing guidelines of how to solve your problem. From that point of view, it is not so much a question of how to do it, but it is a question of somehow letting the panic possess us. Usually what happens is that when the panic arises, we try to brush it off and occupy ourselves with something else. It's like the traditional situation of a wife panicking and then the husband trying to calm down his freaky wife and make her feel secure. There is somebody very reasonable in us, who says, "This is your imagination. Everything is going to be okay. Don't worry. Take a rest. Have a glass of milk." But if rather than taking this approach, you somehow go along with the panic and become the panic, there is a lot of room in the panic, because the panic if full of air bubbles, so to speak. It is very spacious—crackling all the time. It is very spacious and somewhat unpleasant on the surface, but, you know, it could be a real thing. So you probably find yourself suspended in the midst of panic, which is suspended in space. It sounds like a Coke ad!

STUDENT: When one finds oneself in an irritating or uncomfortable situation, does one stay with one particular style through that whole situation, or does the style change from moment to moment? Or does it change along with each new problematic situation?

TRUNGPA RINPOCHE: It depends which particular area you are relating to. Sometimes it changes very speedily and sometimes it remains very solid. But it depends on your reference point.

S: On the type of problem that arises?

TR: Yes, on the type of problem that arises *and* also your reference point in the outside world coming back to you and how that relates with the whole situation. Usually, you act in accordance with that; you reshape your style.

S: Is everything simply conditioned by situations then? We have no personality, and after the basic split we simply produce the five types of responses in reaction to situations?

TR: We are not just shaped by situations. Somehow there is also an element present that is ignoring the basic ignorance at the same time. If you were purely reacting in accordance with the situation, if you didn't have a personality, when would you learn lessons? If you couldn't learn anything, you would simply be reacting to situations all the time. You would just bounce around like a ping-pong ball. You couldn't develop egohood; you couldn't become anything. You would just bounce around until you die, and even afterward . . . (well, we don't know about that).

S: My idea was not that there was no intelligence, but rather no particular style.

TR: Style is intelligence. You begin to accumulate information about when you went wrong and how you can go right. You build up a record of that, and then as you become more experienced, you become a professional. In fact, at that point, somebody else can come to you and consult you. You can give professional advice on how to handle situations. It may be that this is only an expression of ignorance at the professional level, but nevertheless there is still some achievement there that takes place.

S: If the style itself is intelligence, and that intelligence is coming from the primordial energy, which is just one energy, I still don't see the time or the place where the variety takes place.

TR: I think there is a misunderstanding there about the primordial intelligence. When we talk about the primordial intelligence on the ego level, ego's primordial intelligence, we are not talking about one intelligence, we are talking about all intelligence. We are not dealing with the one and the many as such, we are talking about all and one at the same time. All and one at the same time.

S: That leads me to a question I've been wondering about. When there is the basic split from the alaya, the basic split that happens in the first skandha, does everybody have their own particular split, or is there one split that created all this?

TR: It's all-encompassing, all big space. You don't exist as one little confused fundamental ego. Your ego is big, gigantic. You have an all-pervasive ego. But somebody else might also have an all-pervasive ego, which is different from yours. I am not saying we are all the children of one ego. We all have our egos, we all have our primordial backgrounds. But each of them is big.

S: So there's an infinite number of alayas.

TR: Sure, yes. That was actually a major subject of debate in tantric philosophy. Certain people said that there is only one alaya, other people said that there are many. That argument went on. But then they finally discovered that there are many alayas.

STUDENT: Rinpoche, in view of the experience of the present moment being all that there is, doesn't it follow that what we call personality or style is really just a collection of memories or echoes of present moments? Wouldn't it then not be an organic thing, but something that is merely dead, in the past, just tracks?

TRUNGPA RINPOCHE: It's possible that there is some memory that makes your trip harden as you go along in your life. It becomes more daring, a more professional trouble-shooter, so to speak. But at the same time, you also depend on certain messages deriving from what actually does exist in life. Those messages tend to feed you, and you put them in the pigeonholes of your memory. But it is not exactly memory as such. It is just a kind of historical feeling preserved in your mind—the bad experience and the good experience. This is not memory in the sense of definite details. You get impressions of things as they are, and then those tend to coincide with what exists in your life situation. Then you feed your memory on those concepts. So the whole thing is built up out of a dream world, a fictional world of some kind.

STUDENT: A lot of statements have been made about the basic split from the alaya, and this sounds very much like the one mind, which I didn't think was part of the Buddhist tradition. Is the alaya the same as the one mind? It would seem that one of them, the alaya, is the ignorant state and the other one, the one mind, is the enlightened state. Are there two sort of basic fields that we oscillate back and forth between? Or is it like in the Hindu tradition where the idea is to become one with the one mind?

TRUNGPA RINPOCHE: Well, if you're theorizing you could dream up a big one mind that everybody is included in. But in terms of experience, which is very real to us, we experience a totality that is our totality. You may find your neighbors still running around in the samsaric battleground while you are experiencing the one mind. They are two entirely different worlds.

We are talking about experience in terms of what happens

now, what is happening at this point to you. You might experience *the* one mind, but it is worthless to talk about whether *the* one mind is someone else's mind or whether you are getting into your own one mind. There's no point in splitting hairs at that point. Particularly since you have achieved the one mind already, you have no desire for further territorializing as to whether this is yours or whether somebody else's mind is also in it, in you.

S: But when people have been talking about splitting from the one, was that referring back to the alaya?

TR: The alaya, yes.

S: Why not from the dharmakaya?

TR: We haven't got to that level yet. We are just talking about halfway through the path, the territory of samsara, which is very personal for us. If we were to talk about dharmakaya that would be fictional. We are talking about the level we can actually experience, or grasp.

3

Instinct and the Mandala Perspective

Let us continue by discussing the nature of the manifestation of emotional patterns that takes place in everyday life. There seems to be some conflict arising from the difference in the way those patterns exist and the way they manifest. We constantly have problems with that. Actually, there is no fundamental problem, but problems arise from the process of our reviewing what happens to us.

The way we exist is very plain and very simple. There is an influx of energies in the form of emotions and occasional flashes of ignorance and stupidity. And when a person is on the path of dharma, there are further occasional flashes of another kind of awareness that is sort of empty-hearted. This awareness takes place at the level where ego does not exist and where you cannot create further trips so as to entertain yourself with a sense of hopefulness. It is a kind of hopelessness that takes place.

As to what manifests, the way in which it manifests is very conditional. We receive some kind of a map, or pattern, some kind of data concerning how things work and how things happen. And at the same time, we try to interpret this. Between receiving the information and interpreting it, we tend to lose something. We tend constantly to exaggerate or miss something, so there is a big gap. Nevertheless, this is another form of truth. It is truth in its falsity, which is *some* kind of reality—we must admit that.

The end result of this whole process is that everything is extraordinarily complicated and detailed. And every bit of this is very meaningful to us. That seems to be the general pattern.

Though this process develops tremendous complexities, these nevertheless manifest in terms of certain forms or styles, all kinds of them. We cannot actually make systematic predictions as to exactly what is going to happen in this process and exactly how it will work; we cannot study the behavior patterns and put all the details down on an information sheet. But there are rough patterns. The only approach seems to be to try to the extent possible to perceive a generalized pattern without trying to interpret every detail.

We also have the distrustful quality of the judgment that goes on at the level of interpretation. The monitor, so to speak, or the commentator, has its tone of voice and its particular manner of expressing things, and its approach is extraordinarily distrustful.

One of the points in the traditional Buddhist way of viewing the question of what reality is or what truth is, is that in fact we cannot perceive reality, we cannot perceive truth. This is not to say that there is no reality or truth, but rather that whatever we perceive, if we happen to perceive anything, we see in accordance with some particular language or approach, and we color it with our own styles and ways of looking at things.

For instance, occasionally we have the experience of no ground, groundlessness, of no substance to our basic ego existence. But that groundlessness, that nonexistence, is not visible. Also, you cannot prove logically that such a thing as nonexistence exists and functions. Once you try to put the nonexistence of ego into systematic language or formulate it in any particular way in order to prove that that nonexistence does exist, this just becomes a greater [expression of] ego, a further way of proving some kind of existence, even though it is in the guise of nonexistence. So the process becomes very complicated and confusing.

Therefore, to realize the mandala perspective at all, we need some kind of aerial point of view, a way of seeing the whole thing totally and completely. In order to have that, we have to be willing to give up the details and the directions.

You might ask, What is left after we give up the details? Well, nothing very much, but at the same time quite a lot. But let us not even get into that question intellectually. It is a question of just doing it.

Understanding the mandala principle is not a matter of getting hold of a good-quality mandala, like the experts who appraise and buy and sell them. A mandala is something that is the product of nonthinking. At the same time, it is a product of enormous feeling, or rather, instinct. The perspective of instinct without logic is the perspective for experiencing the mandala principle.

We come back here to the practice of meditation. Meditation is a man-made thing, naturally; otherwise, there would be no such thing as meditation. It is a man-made version of enlightenment. But at the same time a sense of great ordeal and great hassle is present in the practice of meditation. It is not an easy matter. It is much more difficult not to do anything and just sit than to do something. Yet strangely, from the practice of meditation comes some kind of state of being. We realize a state of being that is utterly hopeless and has no chance of survival. From the practice of meditation, a sense of hopelessness and no chance of survival begins to occur, and sometimes there is even a sense of regression. Then, at some point, we begin to find a kind of a loose end, some area that we haven't covered. That area that we haven't covered is an interesting area. It has the qualities of instinct.

Instinct cannot be overpowered by efficiency. It has to be ripened through a natural organic process. So to come to a realization of the mandala principle, a person must go through the artificiality of something like the technique of meditation. Doing that, a person also begins to go through a sense of disappointment. This tends to bring a lot of space and exaggerate the sense of organicness, of instinct. That is the working basis for beginning our study of mandala and the five buddha principles. It is very important for us to know that this study is very closely linked with practice and that it involves a lot of discipline.

STUDENT: Is the mandala principle a process, or is it that you understand the mandala principle after you go through the artificial process of meditation and the disappointment and the coming to instinct?

TRUNGPA RINPOCHE: The understanding of it is maybe a process. The product of the understanding is self-existent. It is like digging up a treasure from the ground. The treasure is there already. The digging process is an organic one; it involves work and labor. Then once you have dug the treasure up, it's there. From that point of view, the process is just temporary.

STUDENT: I don't understand what a mandala is. I know it is not just the pictures in the books. Is it the imagery of that process you just described?

TRUNGPA RINPOCHE: We have the symbolism of the mandala and we have the basic principle of the mandala. As a basic principle, mandala is that which is contained in everyday life. That includes the animate and the inanimate, form and the formless, emotion and nonemotion. Wherever there is relationship, that seems to be the mandala principle—wherever there is connection with any kind of reference point. I am not speaking of reference point at the conceptual level, but of reference point on the level of things as they are. For example, light and darkness are not influenced by concepts, particularly, but are a natural organic thing. Whenever there is this kind of reference point, there is mandala principle.

Mandala literally means "group," "society," "organization," that which is interlinked. It is like the notion of an accumulation of lots of single details, which, put together, make a whole. In the books, it is described as like a yak's tail. There are lots of single hairs that make up the tail, but what you see is a big bundle of hair, which constitutes a yak's tail. You cannot separate each hair out of it.

STUDENT: You talked about giving up details and direction and having an aerial perspective. It seems to me that that might get tricky. One might get stuck in ignorance or some kind of zombie state.

TRUNGPA RINPOCHE: The point here seems to be that if you are already at the ignorance level, you have nothing to give up, because you are not aware of the details in any case. Whereas if you do have something to give up, that is to say, if you have developed some kind of awareness of the existence of details, then you bypass or transcend it. This actually makes the details more real. The more you give up, the more they arise. And you cannot give it up just like that; it's not possible. Constant practice is needed.

S: Would that somehow be related to, in working with emotions, trying not to make use of them but just letting them take you over. Or in dealing with panic, just letting it take you over. Would it mean not being concerned with this and that with regard to the emotions, not trying to do something with them or give them direction? Would that be like an aerial point of view in regard to the emotions?

TR: Yes, I suppose, to some extent. But letting them take you over here would not so much mean purely becoming subject to them. Then they would not be taking over but invading. That would be an inward direction rather than an outward direction. On the other hand, if you suppress them, that would also be a process of rejecting. So I suppose it is a question of completely letting be. That way, the emotions can function freely, free from any burden whatsoever, from anywhere, physically and psychologically. Then they function in a way traditionally described as like a cloud arising in the sky and then dissolving. Letting be in this way is not exactly just doing nothing; it is also a way of experiencing the emotions. Unless you let them be as they are, you cannot experience them.

S: What one gives up is the tendency to do something with them?

TR: Yes, that's right. Once you begin to do something with them, there's no freedom. It is imprisonment—you are imprisoned by them.

STUDENT: How does the freedom you just described relate to the freedom you were talking about before? You said that the way the five buddha principles relate to the basic ignorance is a kind of freedom, a freedom of being able to move around because of being totally with the ignorance. How does that relate to the freedom you were just describing of letting things be?

TRUNGPA RINPOCHE: I think it's the same thing. Is there any problem?

S: I'm just somehow very confused. I'm trying to put things together and—

TR: Well, I wouldn't try to put things together too neatly.

STUDENT: Could you explain a little further what you mean by "instinct"? Is it like what animals are considered to have— just doing the appropriate thing automatically? Or is it something else?

TRUNGPA RINPOCHE: Instinct in this case is not purely a physical or biological effect that reflects onto the state of awareness or state of mind. Instinct here is an experience in which you feel that you are completely adequate, that you do not need the aid of conventional logic or any proof of anything. It is a sense of a first-hand account, first-hand experience, actually experiencing. At that point, you do not watch yourself experiencing, you simply just do experience. It is very straightforward. The closest traditional analogy, which a lot of people like the siddhas Saraha and Tilopa have used, is that of a mute man tasting sweetness, intense sweetness. It is delicious to taste. The mute has a real taste of this sweetness, he tastes it magnificently, but he can't describe it because he is mute. Muteness here refers to the absence of intellectualizing, of describing the details and facets of this sweet taste. It is a total experience. This is quite different from animal instinct, which is driven by conditions or physical situations or relationship to physical situations. In this case, it is a first-hand account of things as they are.

STUDENT: You were talking about the gap that occurs between the receiving of the data and the interpretation of it. You said that the interpretation was false but that there was a truth in that falsity. Could you say more about that? It is inevitable that that discrepancy will be there, isn't it? That discrepancy is there in every case, right?

TRUNGPA RINPOCHE: I think so, yes, definitely. It is not a question of trying to avoid that. Things do happen that way. That kind of gap is there. One has to develop a sort of overview of the whole thing. Then quite possibly there would be the tendency to not separate between the way things are and the way they manifest. Both become the same thing. That does not mean that that will free you from the second type of thing [the interpretation] happening. It will still happen in any case. But the idea is that some kind of trust begins to develop somewhere, trust that even though there is a gap, it doesn't matter.

S: Is that the same idea as what you were saying about overlooking the details, or rather taking an overall view of them? You said that to see the mandala, you would have to overlook the details and adopt an aerial perspective.

TR: Yes, that's it. Yes. Because if you begin to see the way it manifests, there are a lot of details in that.

STUDENT: You used the phrase "empty-hearted awareness." Could you say more about what that is?

TRUNGPA RINPOCHE: That is not supposed to be a metaphysical term. It is an experiential expression. It refers to a sense of the rug being pulled out from under your feet, along with a sense of nondwelling—not exactly a sense of floating, but of nondwelling. It's a stillness, not a pulsating, flickering kind of thing. It is as though you have suddenly been exploded and then you dissolve into the atmosphere, slowly. It is sort of an evaporation of something or other.

S: Is this an experience that we are all familiar with?

TR: I hope so. I think it is an experience that is very frequent. Maybe we overlook it or regard it as just not important, but we tend to do that with everything.

STUDENT: Is the gap between our intake of information

and our analysis or understanding of it the gap in which we manifest our particular style in the mandala?

TRUNGPA RINPOCHE: In the gap?

S: Yes.

TR: Not in the gap, but at the borderline where you begin building a bridge over the gap. It is that particular meeting point where you are approaching the gap, the neighborhood of the boundary itself rather than the gap. There is that, and after that there is the manifestation of the mandala.

S: Is meditation essential to becoming aware of how we build that bridge?

TR: Yes. I think meditation is actually the bridge itself. Definitely, yes.

STUDENT: Is what you meant by distrust at the level of the watcher that the watcher clouds our perception of reality?

TRUNGPA RINPOCHE: Yes. It also gets the wrong information. Either it misses the point or exaggerates something.

S: And the watcher is also the beginning of the path, that which begins to allow us to see the confusion.

TR: Yes.

S: And then the trust that we develop is being willing to sit in the gap when the watcher isn't . . .

TR: Not necessarily. It is to see the futility of the watcher rather than to appreciate the gap. It is to see the activities of the watcher and how it works, how it functions.

STUDENT: I remember your saying somewhere that emotions are not really different from thoughts, that they're a special kind of thought that we give a lot of prestige to, but now you seem to be implying that they are something distinct.

TRUNGPA RINPOCHE: Emotions are sort of colors that exist in the thoughts, rather than being a special species, so to speak. They are the highlights of thoughts, which according to tradition have five colors—white, blue, yellow, red, and green. Traditionally, there are these five types of emotions which are five types of exaggerated thoughts. But they have a particular energy.

STUDENT: Rinpoche, you mentioned a feeling of a loss of ground and of regression. Times like those are times when you least have trust in your own intelligence to deal with the situation. Is regular meditation practice enough to deal with that, or is some other effort necessary?

TRUNGPA RINPOCHE: We are speaking very generally. I think we need meditation as well as meditation-in-action in our everyday lives. Meditation-in-action provides a sense of solidity and sanity as well as willingness to enter into the encounter with life. And that in turn brings up the question of the gap and the neighborhood of energy where the mandala perspective is happening. So we need both. We can't say that sitting practice by itself is the only way. The two have to complement each other.

4

Three Aspects of Perception

We might elaborate further at this point on the idea of relating with the world. To begin with, there are some very tough questions regarding this, such as what is the world and whose world is it, and what does relating with it actually mean.

Basically, it seems to be nobody's world, since there is nobody, as such. The energy that is constantly taking place does not belong to anybody; it is a natural organic process. But on this basis, we function as though the world belongs to us. I function as if I have myself, as if I do exist.

Here the nonexistence of ego is not a philosophical matter, but simply a matter of perception. Perception is unable to trace back its existence [to an origin], so it becomes just sheer energy, without a beginner of the perception and without any substance. It is just simple perception.

Perception on that level has three aspects. The first is perception as experience. In this case, experience does not refer to the experience of self-confirmation, but to experience in the sense of things as they are. White is white, black is black, and so forth.

Then there is [the second aspect], the perception of emptiness, which is the absence of things as they are. Things have their room; things always come along with a certain sense of room, of space. Even though they may appear within the complexities of the overcrowdedness of experience, they provide their own space within the overcrowdedness. Actually, overcrowdedness and room are the same thing; overcrowdedness *is* room in some sense. This is because there is movement involved, because there is dance and play involved. At the same time, there is a shifty and intangible quality, and because of that the whole thing is very lucid.

There is experience, then space or emptiness, and then the final aspect, which is called luminosity. Luminosity has nothing to do with bright visual light. It is a sense of sharp boundary and clarity. There is no theoretical or intellectual reference point for this, but in terms of ordinary experience, it is a sense of clarity, a sense of things being seen as they are, unmistakably.

So there are these three aspects of perception: the sense of experience, the sense of emptiness, and the sense of luminosity. The point is that with that level of perception [that contains the three aspects], one is able to see all the patterns of one's life. Whether the patterns of one's life are regarded as neurotic or enlightened, one is able to see them all clearly. That seems to be the beginning of some glimpse of the mandala perspective, the beginning of a glimpse of the five buddha energies.

In other words, the five types of energies are not confined to the level of the enlightened state alone. They are also contained in the confused level. The point is to see them as they are—thoroughly confused, thoroughly neurotic, and thoroughly painful; or extraordinarily pleasurable, extraordinarily expansive, joyous, and humorous—whatever. So we are not trying to remove what we perceive; we are not trying to reshape the world according to how we would like to see it.

We are seeing the world as it is without reshaping. Whatever comes along in us is part of the buddha principles and part of the mandala setup.

I would like to remind you once again that the approach we are taking here is purely an experiential approach. We are not talking about things from a philosophical point of view, discussing whether such-and-such a thing exists or not; we are not trying to see how this fits into a conceptual framework of phenomenological experience. We are not talking about those things.

Actually, in many cases the philosophers have gone wrong by trying to find out the truth of the matter concerning the way things are, rather than relating with things in terms of perception. As a result, they find themselves completely theorizing the whole thing without knowing what actual experience we might have of things as they are. If we theorize about the existence of the world, its solidity, its eternality, and so on, we block a very large chunk of our own experience, because we are trying too much to prove or establish the foundations [of our philosophical view]. So much so, that we end up concerned with the foundations [of our view] rather than its relationship to the earth. That even seems to be the wrong approach to metaphysics. But in this case we are not talking about metaphysics. We are speaking on the experiential level about what we experience in our everyday life situation, which does not have to be confirmed by theory or proved. It does not depend on anything of that nature. It is simply a matter of everyday experience from minute to minute. It does not involve any long-term projects.

The question of perception becomes very important here, because perception cannot be packed down to form a solid foundation. Perceptions shift and float very much with the experience of life. You might say, "I saw a beautiful formation of clouds over the Himalayas." That does not mean to say that those clouds will always be there. Even though such cloud formations may be among the attributes of looking at the Himalayas, you would not expect necessarily always to see a beautiful cloud formation when you get to the Himalayas. You might arrive in the middle of the night or when the sky is completely clear.

When you describe your experience to somebody else, whatever you perceived at a particular moment may sound extremely full and vivid and fantastic, because somehow you have managed to convey the experience of that moment. But if you try to recapture that experience and mimic the whole thing all over again, that is quite impossible. Quite possibly, you might end up philosophizing about it and getting further and further away from reality, so to speak, whatever that is.

There is a sharp precision that exists in our life, which generally arises from some form of training and discipline, particularly the sitting practice of meditation. Not that the sitting practice of meditation sharpens our perception, but sitting practice makes it possible for us to perceive sharply. It is a question of removing the clouds rather than of recreating the sun. That seems to be the whole point.

There is some faint experience of reality—it seems to be very faint and uncertain. But however faint it may be, it is still very sharp and precise and tends to bring a lot of clarity also. On the whole, this kind of perception we are talking about depends on a certain kind of watchfulness. This watchfulness is not particularly being careful or tiptoeing. This watchfulness is experiencing a sudden glimpse—of whatever—without any qualifications: just the sudden glimpse itself.

This point has led to problems and is regarded as enigmatic. If we say, "You should see a sudden glimpse," people usually ask, "Of what?" And if we do not have anything to say about what it is, then the whole thing is regarded as absurd. But if we could change our thinking style entirely, if we could open our mind to something slightly more than what we have already been told, then we could step beyond the level where everything is purely based on the idea of a business transaction and a profit-making process. There are possibilities of awareness without any conditions, conditions in this case being the sense that you might be able to get something out of it, the sense that you are going to be able to see certain particular things with this awareness. It is just simple straightforward awareness of itself—awareness being aware without anything being put in it. That kind of perception seems to be the only key point. It is the key perspective, the microscope that makes it possible to perceive the three types of perception we discussed.

On that level, [perceiving] the spectrum of the mandala of the five buddha principles is no big deal. Those principles are not an extraordinary thing to perceive. Perceiving them is quite matter-of-fact. The basic mandala principle becomes very simple. It is just simply that everything is related with everything else. It is quite simple and straightforward.

STUDENT: Could you say something more about perception as experience?

TRUNGPA RINPOCHE: Maybe you could try to say something about it. Just try guesswork.

S: Is it perception of your subjective experience as it's going on, even though you admit that it's subjective?

TR: Getting close, yes. But there is something else that is needed for that.

S: To be experiencing things.

TR: Yes, but when you're experiencing something, what comes with it?

S: Reactions? Your own reactions?

TR: Yes, but what is that reaction called?

S: Experience?

TR: No, there's something else.

S: Emotions?

TR: You're getting close.

S: Thoughts? Perceptions?

TR: Not necessarily.

S: Responses?

TR: The driving force of responses, yes.

S: So it's . . .

TR: It's energy. You see, there is a kind of exuberant energy that goes with perception and experience. When you experience something, you actually recapture what you experience. For example, when you say, "I have seen a piece of shit," it is very vivid and real, and you catch that energy. Or, "I have seen the naked sun." There is a lot of energy behind that. You actually experience it as though you are it. You almost become indivisible from something at the moment when you experience it. It is that kind of direct communication without anything in between.

S: So it's really throwing yourself in totally.

TR: It doesn't require throwing, particularly. It is realized on the spot.

STUDENT: The clarity that you speak of, is that always related to a sense of spaciousness?

TRUNGPA RINPOCHE: I think so, yes. Otherwise there's no sharpness. If there were no space, it would be unfocused.

S: Do we all start as luminous beings and then forget our luminosity?

TR: Luminous beings? Sounds like Don Juan.

S: Do we start as luminous and forget our luminosity?

TR: It is not a question of starting as luminous—we are. Even while uncertainties are taking place, we *are* still. What we are talking about is just a way of looking again and focusing on it. It is not a matter of a case history, particularly; it's an ongoing thing. Right at this moment, we are luminous and we are empty and we are perceptive at the same time.

STUDENT: I believe you said earlier that when you perceive something, something is either lost or exaggerated. Is it through the interpretation of the perception that this happens?

TRUNGPA RINPOCHE: Yes.

S: It's not the perception itself that creates the exaggeration?

TR: [It happens] once you begin to conceptualize, once you begin to elaborate on it.

S: But just the perception itself is still very accurate. So are perception and experience equal in that sense?

TR: Perception is experience if you are *there*. But perception cannot be experience if you are not there.

S: If you include yourself in the perception.

TR: There's no self to include.

S: Is the sense that we have of a self perceiving, itself a perception? I'm talking about the sense of selfhood that I experience in confronting reality, as if I'm a corporation that has to deal with what's around me. Is that a perception?

TR: No, because that needs second thoughts to confirm it. The actual perception is the first thought.

S: How do we know if we can trust our perceptions?

TR: If you know that there's no "we" as such, then it seems to go very smoothly.

S: Well, how do I know if I can trust my perceptions?

TR: You can reword it any way you want; it's still the same thing.

S: Well, how can you tell the difference between perception and projection?

TR: In the case of a projection, you're waiting for something to bounce back and confirm your existence. Perception is just sort of an antenna that exists.

S: It seems you are saying that the confusion, or distortion, of perceptions arises from the perceiver wanting to do something with the perception, wanting to act somehow on what he or she is perceiving. Does the primitive confusion you spoke of at the beginning arise from the same source?

TR: That is what we are talking about, yes. When we talk about it as ego or self, we are talking about that primordial one, that primeval state of this*ness,* or solid fixation. So, yes, we are talking about that.

S: You've talked about this primordial sense of thisness as some sort of nonconceptual reference point and have said that the mandala principle exists whenever there is a reference point. Is this sense of thisness the same type of reference point from which the mandala principle or perspective springs?

TR: It gets a little complicated in that area. There is a twist there, which is that when there is a reference point, that is a kind of primitive belief; then you realize that there is actually no one to react to that reference point, and that brings you to a different or higher level altogether. Both levels are active ingredients in the realization of the mandala principle. But [we have to be clear that] we are talking about two levels at the same time: the primitive or primordial ego and the realization of the nonexistence of the reactor to that.

S: Not solidifying that . . .

TR: Yes, not solidifying that solidification, so to speak.

S: You say that with that level of perception, the mandala principle is a simple sense of connections?

TR: Yes.

S: And you've spoken before about trusting the karmic reality of cause and effect. Is that related to the sense of connection?

TR: Yes, because that is the ultimate karmic cause and effect, that of no action. It is the highest form of karma, *akarma,* nonkarma.

S: Are the connections of the mandala principle in this nonkarma?

TR: Fundamentally, although as far as the expressions are concerned, there may be various styles. But those expressions are based on certain fundamentals that make it possible for the mandala principle to come and go and manifest itself in different fashions.

STUDENT: You talked about recounting an experience, a real perception, without losing the energy of it. It seems to me that that is what underlies a work of art. It's the ability to hold onto the energy even though the experience is in the past—a kind of working that is not ego-based but is very positive. Does that seem like a possible interpretation?

TRUNGPA RINPOCHE: I think the point here is that you can work on both levels at once: the level of the ego-based world with its energies, emotions, and so on; and the non-ego-based level. There is no conflict between the two, for the very fact that they are organically linked somehow. The non-ego-based level is more refined. The ego-based level is a crude form of that.

S: So you don't try to cut them off from each other and keep one and throw the other out.

TR: No, not at all. It's very natural from that point of view.

S: It sounds to me like perception of experience, perception of emptiness, and perception of luminosity are successively deeper layers of the same thing. Is that the case?

TR: I think you see all three of them at once, but with different accents on them, depending on the mood of the reality of the time.

S: You've spoken about the gap before. We've discussed and thought about it a lot, and I'm still confused. I previously thought you meant that the gap was that time when you are directly experiencing something. You are not interpreting or laying anything on the experience; you are just right there, so there is a gap in your normal sense of awareness, because your normal sense of awareness is based on the continuity of interpretations and commentaries. But when you talked about the gap earlier on here, you talked about it as that space that is between your direct experience and your interpretation in which you lose or exaggerate something. I was wondering if perhaps you could clarify that.

TR: I think we are talking about two different ways of looking at things. There is a contrast here between the mahayana teaching of shunyata, which is a gap; and the tantric view of gap, or the mandala principle. Those two are slightly different. According to the tantric teachings, the realization takes place in the moment when the boundary occurs, because you are working with the energy rather than purely working with the absence of something. You are not trying to see everything as empty as such, but you are trying to see everything as transmutable energy. And the transformation takes place at just that point when you reach the boundary.

S: Just when you reach the boundary of what?

TR: The gap is just a shift between two reference points. In this case, the gap is not particularly a big deal, like the shunyata experience. It's just a gap with a small *g*. It's a shift, a change. There's just a journey and you reach halfway between this and that, which is not particularly a shunyata type of experience. I wouldn't say that the gap has the quality of emptiness. It is just going away from somewhere and arriving at some other situation. If you combine this with the mahayana's experience of shunyata, then the experience of shunyata is included in the boundary. According to the vajrayana, the shunyata experience is actually in the boundary rather than particularly in the gap.

[Even in the mahayana,] the shunyata symbolism is that of a mother who gives birth. It is connected with the mother principle, the creator. So the idea here is that the creator is the boundary—the shunyata experience gives birth to the boundary. Here the gap has more energy in it than the mahayana version of just shunyata, emptiness alone. Here shunyata is something to play with. Finally, shunyata finds a playmate, a lover, and therefore becomes more dynamic than the straight version, the straight, simple mahayana version where everything is transcended.

S: It seems, then, that the mahayana shunyata is an incomplete perception, something unreal created by the practitioner. If shunyata is really in the boundary where there's lots of energy, the mahayana shunyata would be just a man-made thing.

TR: You can't say that exactly. If you are in it, you feel very complete. This approach contains a reference to further realities, so to speak. The very fact that more emphasis is put on transcendence creates a sense of still overcoming, still going beyond. Whereas in the vajrayana, going beyond is not important; the boundary, or the ridge, itself is important, rather than going beyond it. So it's not getting inside the room from outside that is important; it's not a question of climbing over the doorstep to get inside. It's the doorstep itself that is important in the vajrayana. The boundary itself is very important, and it does not refer to transcending anything, particularly. It is regarded as energy rather than as an obstacle.

S: Why do we need the mahayana conception of shunyata? Why don't we just try dealing with the boundary from the beginning?

TR: The boundary is regarded as an obstacle from the mahayana point of view. In the mahayana, you can only overcome the notion of the boundary by using the experiential logic that the inside of the boundary is the same as the outside of the boundary and that therefore there is no boundary— rather than regarding the boundary itself as a great thing.

S: So is it necessary to go through the mahayana version of shunyata before indulging in—

TR: The interesting point is that, although we may be talking about the vajrayana version of shunyata on the linguistic level, we might still be perceiving in a purely mahayana fashion. You can't just suddenly make a policy change. It depends on the level of one's growth.

STUDENT: Earlier you said that meditation is a bridge over the gap. If the gap is important, why would you want to bridge it?

TRUNGPA RINPOCHE: To make the whole thing into a big boundary rather than having a gap.

S: With the bridge the gap itself becomes obsolete?

TR: The bridge is the boundary, so you have a very thick

boundary, rather than there being a gap and then you come to a no-man's land and then to somebody else's land. That's the way it happens in Texas anyway.

S: I am confused, because when you were talking about the mahayana symbolism of shunyata, you seemed to say both that the mother, or the creator, is the boundary and that she gives birth to the boundary.

TR: Well, if you are relating to that, you are the boundary maker as well as the boundary itself.

S: Oh, I see. The tantrics by not making that differentiation—

TR: That's right.

5

A Glimpse of the Five Buddha Families

Having discussed the three aspects of perception, we could perhaps go on to a more elaborate level of experience than that discussed in connection with them. Perceptions are a kind of kindling wood that brings us to a certain state of awareness of experience, which then becomes the experience of what is known as *isness*. This is a particular term that has been developed as part of the Buddhist vocabulary. I have not seen it used in this way anywhere else. In terms of actual experience, starting with perception, isness is the experience of things as they are, but not only that: that experience also confirms itself by itself. So we see things as they are—or maybe I should say, as they is—and then isness comes from seeing it as it is and tasting it.

In tantric language, this particular taste is known as *one taste* or *one flavor*. When we talk about one flavor, we do not mean abandoning everything but one particular situation and developing an allegiance to that particular one thing among many. It has nothing to do with there being a lack of many and therefore we happen to end up with one. It has nothing to do with making a choice or rejecting something else. In fact, it is the opposite: because there are no rejections, it is possible to stick with that one, which means all.

We have already talked about [the way in which] all and one could be similar. When we talk about many, generally it means covering many areas, accumulating a lot of stuff, a lot of pieces of information. But when we talk about all, that automatically means covering a large portion of the atmosphere of a situation. In this case, we are talking about a greater-area atmosphere, which is a state of experience of the world of reality.

[Ordinarily,] reality can be qualified by giving it various functions. But in this case, there is no function, there are no qualifications. All we can speak of here is nakedness, unclothedness. It is experience that is free from the clothing of conventionality, free from the clothing of relative truth. It is also free from all the other things that come from that—ego-orientation, orientation toward security, and orientation toward eternity.

Eternity here is the sense that one's life can last forever. We hope that any kind of spiritual experience we might be able to have will make it worth living longer and might also help us to live longer. We hope that we will be able to live longer and longer and longer, that we will be able to survive eternally without having to face the truth of death. But this is a kind of simpleminded approach that I do not think is worth discussing at this point.

Beyond the level of that primitive approach, there is a sense of experiencing reality in its true nakedness—but not for any particular purpose. The conventional question at this point is, "Having discovered this, what am I going to get out of it? What is going to happen to me?" But the truth of the matter seems to be, nothing is going to happen to you. That's it. There is nothing more. If I have disappointed you, I'm sorry, but we cannot do anything about it. That's things as they are, or things "as it hangs."

So we make successive attempts to get to unqualified experience, realization without any tail attached to it, without any confirmation or promises attached to it. And then we might begin to accept things as they are in a really simple, ordinary way; we will probably be able to perceive some glimpse of reality without conditions. At that point, we might say that we are experiencing the five types of buddha intelligence.

I am sure you have already heard and read a great deal about the five buddha families.

The five types of buddha principles are not a Buddhist version of astrology. They have nothing to do with fortune-telling or finding the strength of the head line in your palm. They are more a guideline to experience in relation to those reference points—or rather, non–reference points—that we have been discussing. They are connected with a realization of phenomena in the complete sense.

We know that everybody has their particular innate style and approach based on the five buddha qualities. For that matter, this is at the same time a person's particular buddha potential in terms of emotions and confusions. But there is also another way of looking at the whole process [related to the five buddha principles]. It is a question of depth and of expansiveness from the depth, which [two factors] can also be seen as simultaneous. In this approach, there is no allegiance to a certain particular buddha principle that you cherish as your one and only style. That [kind of partial] view would tend to give us a two-dimensional experience of the buddha principles. In order to see the whole thing in terms of a three-dimensional experience, we have to approach it from depth to expansion, or concentration to expansion.

In relating to our state of being or experience at the level of transcending concepts, we can regard the five principles as various depths, various levels of depth. These are also various degrees of heaviness, or weight. If something is floating in water, part of it is going to be most prominent. Part of it is going to be floating closest to the surface, and part of it is going to be at the greatest depth in the ocean. That depends on the heaviness or lightness of the substance. In this case, it is the same approach. And from that point of view, whenever we function, we function with all five principles at once. We cannot deny this, despite our particular [predominant] characteristic that might exist.

This brings a different perspective on one-pointedness—a vertical rather than a horizontal one. You start with the buddha-family buddha principle, which is the heaviest of all. It is the most solid material, that which clings to ego or relates to a sense of all-pervasive spaciousness, the wisdom of all-pervasive space. This is the core of the matter, the core of the whole thing. It is that which brings a sense of solidity and a sense of basic being, a sense of openness and a sense of wisdom and sanity at the same time. That is the buddha buddha family, which is correlated with the skandha of form, which is the most basic.[1]

From there, you begin to move out slowly to the experience of feeling. This derives from the solidity of the awakened state of mind and brings a sense of expansiveness, intelligent expansiveness, like tentacles or antennae of all kinds. You begin to relate with areas of relationship very clearly and fully and thoroughly. This is related with the ratna buddha family.

The next one is impulse, which is connected with the padma family, because of its sharpness and quickness, and at the same time the willingness to seduce the world outside into your reference point, into relationship with you. Even in the awakened state of this principle, there is a willingness to communicate, to relate. This padma-family principle is much lighter than the previous two.

The fourth one is concept, which is connected with the karma family. This principle happens very actively and very efficiently. Any activity or efficiency that takes place in your state of being is related with the karma-family process.

We are rising out of the depths of the ocean. As we float we are slowly approaching the surface.

The fifth one is consciousness, which is the vajra family. Here there is a type of intelligence and intellect that operates with very minute precision and clarity, so the whole thing becomes extraordinarily workable. Once you are on the surface, you know how to relate with the phenomenal world and you know what the working basis of the phenomenal world is. In terms of the activity of a buddha, there are always skillful means for relating appropriately with the reference points of perceivers of the teaching. A buddha will know how to treat students, how to speak in their own terms, their own language, and relate in terms of their own style in a very sharp, penetrating, and precise fashion.

So the five skandhas are part of our basic makeup, of our being, both from the samsaric and nirvanic points of view. Therefore, we are constantly manifesting the five types of buddha-nature within ourselves directly and precisely with a certain amount of style. It is very important to realize that, because of that, the five types of energy are completely available to us and workable. We can relate with them very precisely, and there are no particular problems attached to that.

Everything seems to be a matter of stepping out from depth to openness, concentration to openness. The five stages of the skandhas are always part of our basic makeup, part of our basic style. We actually operate from those grounds, from those basic styles constantly, all the time. We have a reference point, whether as part of a meditative state or a confused one. We start from that basic reference point and begin to expand toward the workabilities of reality, depending on whatever challenges or promises come up for us. That is the general pattern that is all-pervasive and prominent.

STUDENT: In the first lecture, you talked about the basic BLAH, or the alaya. The "thisness" of it seems to be related to the first skandha and the buddha family. Is there some close connection?

TRUNGPA RINPOCHE: The buddha buddha family as we are talking about it is beyond all, beyond alaya and beyond what might be known as nirvana. Of course, there is a reference point connected with it, just as our life is partly connected with the night and partly connected with the day.

S: Is the buddha family one taste? Is that why it's the heaviest—because it's reaching the sense of "isness"?

TR: That's right. It's one taste.

S: And from there, it is a process of expansion?

TR: Yes. It is one taste not in the sense of a monotone, but in the sense of—

S: Yes, that's exactly why it expands.

TR: Yes, yes. That's right.

STUDENT: Rinpoche, tonight you seemed to talk a lot about acceptance, about isness and accepting things as they are. I remember once hearing you say that life was like a straight drink without any watering down, and I wonder if the Buddhist path amounts to ever greater degrees of being able to accept what is. It seems almost like going to a horror movie where you keep wanting to run out because of the phenomena that you see. Is it just a matter of getting used to what you see so you don't need to run out?

TRUNGPA RINPOCHE: "Getting used to it" meaning what?

S: Getting used to your insight.

TR: Well, if you go to a horror movie, you usually don't want to run out, because you want to get your money's worth. It's partially entertaining even though you might detest the whole thing. We usually stick with it unless we are cowardly or sleepy or sick or something. Usually people with any sense of fun or sense of ironic vigor will stay and watch and try to finish the whole thing. The point is, one taste is like a straight drink, obviously. But at the same time, it's not so much a matter of acceptance or yielding as such. I think the whole thing boils down to understanding that you can't actually dictate [what happens], you can't change your phenomena, not because you finally find it hopeless and give up trying, but because relating to the phenomenal world becomes very straightforward and direct.

S: Is that because of the egolessness that is derived from being able to perceive the world?

TR: I think so, yes. It is like nobody, really at the bottom of their heart, complains that there is day and night. Accepting that transcends giving up, because it is already such a daily occurrence.

STUDENT: In *Cutting Through Spiritual Materialism*, you describe the five buddha families as in the center and in the east, south, west, and north. Your description just now was much more like concentric circles, and the families seemed much more one with each other than here and there. It doesn't seem like the same thing.

TRUNGPA RINPOCHE: This approach is not exactly the same, but it arrives at the same principle. It's like a tree. You study the roots underground, and then above the ground you have the trunk, then slowly you get to the top and you study the branches and fruit and blossoms and all the kinds of leaves. It's that kind of approach, rather than having everything divided into quarters or provinces.

STUDENT: It sounds like the buddha buddha family has more depth to it. You said it was weightier. And then as you talked about the buddha families, the vajra family sounded more surfacy, as though there's less to it, less quality to it.

TRUNGPA RINPOCHE: Yes. The vajra is more expansive, and the buddha is very deep, concentrated.

S: Is that like with the five skandhas: You start with the grain of sand and by the time you reach the fifth skandha, it's a total deterioration? And here, by the time you get to the vajra family, it's like a deterioration from the buddha family, which has more depth to it?[2]

TR: From the samsaric point of view, that is the case, I think. But you can't completely rely on that outlook, because you would be trying to regroup yourself every minute. There is a constant expanding and contracting, expanding and contracting—the game goes on all the time.

6

Sambhogakaya Buddha

There are two basic points I would like to touch on by way of conclusion. Those two points are the state of awareness that comes through sitting meditation and the sense of appreciation that goes with it. That awareness is able to perceive the workings of the phenomenal world as the five buddha principles and the mandala setup, and the appreciation brings an understanding of the magical aspect of that.

This awareness is the unconditional awareness that we have discussed already. It is awareness without purpose or goal, without aim. From that awareness, a state of fearlessness arises, and through that fearlessness, the workings of phenomena become self-existing magic. In this case, magic is not conjuring up demons or playing tricks. It is magic in the sense that the phenomenal world possesses a sense of enormous health and strength—wholesomeness. From that sense of strength and wholesomeness, a person is able to nourish himself. And a person is also able to contribute further nourishment to the phenomenal world at the same time. So it is not a one-way journey but a two-way exchange.

That exchange of nourishment, which is basic sanity, and the sense of fearlessness bring the state of awareness back. So a constant circle of exchange takes place. And it becomes enjoyable. It is not that one enters into a state of euphoria or anything like that, but still, it is basically enjoyable, because the sharp edges, which are doubt and uncertainty, begin to dissolve. This brings an almost supernatural quality, an unexpected excitement. One is able to mold such a world into a pattern, not from the point of view of desire and attachment and anxiety, but from the point of view of life and fearlessness of death.

The whole thing takes place, as we said earlier, on the basis of empty-heartedness. You don't exist and the energy doesn't exist and the phenomenal world doesn't exist, therefore everything *does* exist. And there is an enormous magical quality about that. It is completely lucid, but at the same time tangible in some sense, because there is texture and the absence of texture. There is a sense of journey and a sense of discrimination, and there is a sense of passion and aggression and everything. But it seems that everything operates on the level of no-ground, which makes the whole operation ideal, so to speak.

The traditional term that applies here is *sambhogakaya buddha*. The sambhogakaya buddha is a manifestation of energy that operates on the level of joy, enjoyment. We could say in some sense that it is the level of transcendental indulgence. This makes life continuous, but not eternal like a brick wall that has been extended from one end of the world to the other. It would not be as solid as that. There would be continuity like that of a flowing brook. The discontinuity becomes continuity and the flow sort of dances as it goes along.

So that is the basic way to view the mandala and the five buddha principles. It is a positive world, not in the sense of a simpleminded love-and-light approach, but in the sense that the world is workable. One can relate with such a world, because everything is visible and very vivid. That dispels hesitation and fear, and you can remold things. You can reshape the clouds and ride on the rainbow. Impossibilities can be achieved by not achieving.

The point is not so much that in reaching such a point we have made progress or made a switch from something else. Rather, it is that we have made the discovery that such experience does exist, such a setup exists all the time. Therefore, it is matter of discovery rather than progress.

STUDENT: What you were saying about the tantrikas making the whole thing boundary and also the tantric idea of continuity or indestructible energy that is always there—those things seem to me to undermine the basic Buddhist idea of impermanence and rising and falling. Is there some change of perception there that goes further than the rising and falling?

TRUNGPA RINPOCHE: Well, at the beginning, at the hinayana level, you become homeless, anagarika. You give up your home, you give up your possessions, power, wealth, and so on. You renounce everything. Naropa even gave up his intellect. Then in tantric practice, the tantrikas repossess what has been given up in an entirely different way. Homelessness becomes being a householder and giving up power becomes the acquisition of greater power. From that point of view, giving up or transcending the flow and setting one's boundary at discriminating awareness is another kind of freedom, but freedom with guts, so to speak. We are more involved with realities, rather than purely dwelling on motivation alone, which seems to be the approach of the earlier yanas. In the earlier yanas your motivation is more important than what you actually experience; and what you experience is often looked upon as something fishy or untrustworthy. One is constantly coming back, pulling oneself back to the motivation and working to purify from that angle. But in tantra, there is a further twist. From the tantric point of view, motivation is just a concept, just a shadow, and what you actually experience apart from the motivation becomes more important. So it is a different twist, repossessing the same thing in a more daring way. And somehow the boundaries seem to be necessary. In order to extend your boundary, you have to have a boundary.

STUDENT: I am trying to understand what one flavor is about. You say that nothing is permanent but impermanence, and nothing is continuous but discontinuity. Now that might tend to give a nihilistic feeling that there is just nothing at all that has any qualities that are retained. But is the point of one flavor that actually relativity has a quality that you get to know or that discontinuity has a certain style or feeling that is always there?

TRUNGPA RINPOCHE: Definitely. In order to be discontinuous, you have to have the strength to be one. Yes.

S: So discontinuity has a personality in a sense, or a feeling.

TR: Yes, there is definitely a texture—

S: —that's always there. That's the one flavor?

TR: Yes. That is why the nonexistence spheres, or realms, such as vajradhatu and dharmadhatu can be defined. They have a name and they have an experience. They are levels that are tangible in some sense. The idea of the analogy of holding a vajra is that the shunyata experience can be handled.

STUDENT: In your description of experience earlier, it sounded as though things get clearer and sharper the more one is able to perceive unconditional reality, and then everything is a sort of luminosity. Things become very clear, and at that point the sharp edges begin to dissolve. Is that a perceptual experience?

TRUNGPA RINPOCHE: The idea of luminosity is not so much a matter of seeing a great contrast in the sense of the more you see light, the more darkness you see. That approach still has a sense of there being mysterious corners there. What we are saying is that at this point there are no sharp edges anymore. There is no more division. Everything is without a shadow.

S: What happened to the alaya experience that you started out this whole series of talks with? What is happening with that at the level you are talking about now?

TR: I think that disappeared somewhere along the way. The situation seems to be that there is something to begin with, but there's nothing to end up with.

STUDENT: In an earlier seminar, you said that art is giving a hint of an experience rather than laying out the whole thing. I have the feeling that what you have been doing here is just giving a hint. You don't want to give us too much—the whole thing is so condensed! Is there something in that?

TRUNGPA RINPOCHE: I think that is the only way. It seems that descriptions wouldn't be complete. Even if you described everything in great detail, it would still just be a finger painting.

STUDENT: Could you say something more about what you meant by reshaping, or remolding?

TRUNGPA RINPOCHE: We are talking about a different kind of reshaping. It is not reshaping in accordance with a model based on the reference point of ego, or "this." In this case, reshaping is exchange. Whenever there is more exchange between this and that and that and this, then you can control the momentum, because there is no one who is controlling. There is no particular aim and object involved, therefore you can steer the energy flow in certain particular directions. The idea of shape here is a matter of direction rather than something based on a particular model.

S: What would be the basis of that directing then?

TR: Itself. The directions themselves. There's no director, rather the direction is its own self-existing energy.

STUDENT: You said that the alaya goes away at some point. In the beginning of the seminar, you said that samsara and nirvana have the same relationship to the alaya, that it was the background for both of them. What do you mean by the alaya being the background for nirvana as well as samsara?

TRUNGPA RINPOCHE: I think it's the same thing. They both began at the same time.

S: That seems to make nirvana just another version of samsara.

TR: Well, sure. If there were no samsara, then there couldn't be any nirvana, and vice versa.

S: Well, when you talk about awakening and coming to this state of empty-heartedness, is there any nirvana at that point?

TR: Well, when we talk about empty-heartedness, we are not saying that the heart is hollow. We are talking about a nonexistent heart. So I don't think any definition is possible. There's no reference point at that level; there's no reference point there.

S: Well, the reason I asked you the question is because I suspected that the word *nirvana* meant something different from *bodhi,* or enlightenment. But from your answer, it seems that you're saying that at that point the whole idea of path and there being awake and asleep no longer makes any sense, because there's no reference point.

TR: Yes. So be it.

S: Then I still have this question: There is some sense of working back toward alaya, as if there's going to be a more direct experience of the ground of confusion, and that is described as a more immediate experience of ego, if I understand correctly. So you don't talk at that point about a more immediate experience of nonego?

TR: No.

S: So it seems that the whole thing is completely ego, starting with the alaya and going through the whole five skandhas and eight consciousnesses. So from the alaya all the way up to nirvana is completely ego.

TR: Yes. Because of that, there is still a reference point.

S: So to put it vulgarly, nirvana is a trip.

TR: Sure. That's not a new discovery. I think that's putting it very politely.

STUDENT: I think I read some place that you said that karma and ratna are more stable than padma and vajra, that somehow too much vajra becomes karma and too much padma becomes ratna, and too much ratna becomes buddha. There was an impression that somehow padma and vajra are more intangible than karma and ratna. I wonder if it would be helpful to get into that a little bit.

TRUNGPA RINPOCHE: I think you said it.

S: Well, why would karma and ratna be more solid than vajra? Why are vajra and padma more intangible?

TR: I think if you look at the descriptions we gave in the previous talk, you will see that vajra is the final blossom—consciousness—and ratna is one of the first. It is at the beginning level—feeling. It is at the level of being earthbound. I think they [the buddha principles] are necessary prerequisites for each other; they are necessary for each other. You cannot have a tree without a trunk, and you also cannot have a tree without leaves. All of them are necessary. But when the wind blows, the leaves of the tree move first, then the trunk. But you could say that the trunk of the tree is also moved by the wind, through the gesture of the leaves. And for that matter, you could also say that the whole earth shakes. It's a relative situation.

S: In any given situation, is there a particular way in which the energies present themselves? Or are they always just there and when we look we see them?

TR: They present themselves in an appropriate manner, yes, naturally. They react in accordance with the energies that are there. It is very much like elements reacting.

STUDENT: Would you say something about the relationship between the five buddha families and the six realms?

TRUNGPA RINPOCHE: That would require another seminar. Let's save it for next time.

STUDENT: I sometimes hear the ratna family referred to in terms of pride. Is this being proud of your own ignorance and stupidity? Is it a stubborn quality, whereby you can see yourself doing this, but you're so proud of who you are or the way you relate with the world that you actually compliment your own ignorance?

TRUNGPA RINPOCHE: I think you could say that, definitely. The point is that when you create a world of your own, you begin to be very proud of your extension, your offshoot, and that tends to feed you back. And at the same time, there is a slight hesitation and embarrassment. You try to avoid looking at the root of the projection, of that offshoot, and the way to cover it up is further arrogance.

STUDENT: Could you equate the alaya with the gap?

TRUNGPA RINPOCHE: It is a somewhat manufactured gap.

S: So the alaya is manufactured then? Is this the alaya that is after the split of duality, this and that?

TR: It is the sympathetic environment for the split.

S: So the alaya is like an ego version of the dharmakaya.

TR: Something like that. In fact, it could be an ego version of vajradhatu.

STUDENT: Rinpoche, if there is nothing to begin with and nothing to end with, what is happening in between?

TRUNGPA RINPOCHE: Well, it works a little differently than that. It seems there is something to begin with and there is nothing to end with, so I suppose in between, there is the dissipation of something into nothing, which is called "the path."

STUDENT: In our discussion group, we were discussing a possible correlation between your vertical description of the buddha families and the breathing during sitting practice. There is the most solid basic factor, which is the sitting posture, and that would be correlated with the buddha family. And the gradual movement toward dissolution into space with the breath would correlate with the vajra family. Is that so? Is there that kind of macrocosm-microcosm relationship between sitting practice and what you are presenting?

TRUNGPA RINPOCHE: I hope so.

S: In the previous talk, you talked about the movement from the depths of the ocean toward the surface, from which point the phenomenal world is best observed. That's the vajra family. But it seems to me that one is most in touch in the buddha family and that it would be from that position that things would be best observed.

TR: That's the root, and it is a question of how much the root can experience the branches. So if there is an intelligent root, then it ceases to be a root, because it begins to be busy being intelligent and is unable to hold onto its earthiness.

Notes

PART ONE

1. Orderly Chaos

1. Samsara is the round of birth and death and rebirth, characterized by suffering, impermanence, and ignorance. Nirvana is the extinguishing of the causes for samsaric existence—enlightenment.

2. These are the twelve nidanas, the causal links that perpetuate karmic existence. They are conventionally enumerated: ignorance (Sanskrit *avidya*, Tibetan *ma rikpa*), impulsive accumulation (S. *samskara*, T. *duje*), consciousness (S. *vijnana*, T. *nampar shepa*), name and form (S. *nama-rupa*, T. *ming dang suk*), sensation or sense consciousness (S. *shad-ayatana*, T. *kyeche druk*), contact (S. *sparsha*, T. *rekpa*), feeling (S. *vedana*, T. *tsorwa*), craving (S. *trishna*, T. *sepa*), grasping (S. *upadana*, T. *nyewar lenpa*), becoming (S. *bhava*, T. *sipa*), birth (S. *jati*, T. *kyewa*), and old age and death (S. *jara-marana*, T. *gashi*).

3. A mandala is usually represented by a diagram with a central deity, a personification of the basic sanity of buddha nature. The constructed form of a mandala has as its basic structure a palace with a center and four gates in the cardinal directions.

4. Kriya yoga emphasizes purity and the understanding that all

phenomena are inherently pure, naturally sacred, and beyond fixation.

5. Madhyamaka is a mahayana school that emphasizes the doctrine of shunyata. This doctrine stresses that all conceptual frameworks are empty of any "reality."

6. A bodhisattva is one who has committed himself to the mahayana path of compassion and the practice of the six paramitas: generosity (S. *dana*, T. *jinpa*), discipline (S. *shila*, T. *tsultrim*), patience (S. *kshanti*, T. *sopa*), exertion (S. *virya*, T. *tsondru*), meditation (S. *dhyana*, T. *sampten*), and knowledge (S. *prajna*, T. *sherab*). Taking the responsibility of a bodhisattva begins with taking a vow, in the presence of one's teacher, to relinquish—or to attain—one's personal enlightenment in order to work for all sentient beings.

5. The Lubrication of Samsara

1. Dakinis ("sky-goers") are tricky and playful female deities, representing the basic space of fertility out of which the play of samsara and nirvana arises.

2. Dharmadhatu is all-encompassing space, unconditional totality—unoriginating and unchanging—in which all phenomena arise, dwell, and cease. Dharmakaya is enlightenment itself, wisdom beyond any reference point—unoriginated, primordial mind, devoid of content.

6. Totality

1. For this sense of lineal, see the Vidyadhara's reference to a "lineal journey" on p. 66. Lineal here seems to refer to a sequence in which one thing follows the other, an ordinary process. As watcher checks backward and forward in the sequence of a conceptualized process, the sense of maintaining one's solid ground vis-a-vis a spacious boundary could develop. Little "checkings" back and forth to confirm the ground would be the cigarettes exchanged at the border.

2. The wheel of life is a graphic representation of samsaric existence. It is held by Yama, the lord of death.

3. Buddha nature is the enlightened essence inherent in sentient beings.

4. *Prajna* (T. *sherab*, knowledge) is the natural sharpness or awareness that sees, discriminates, and also sees through conceptual discrimination. "Lower prajna" includes any sort of worldly knowledge (how to cook a meal, for example). "Higher prajna" includes two stages: seeing phenomena as impermanent, egoless, and suffering; and a higher prajna that sees a direct knowledge of things as they are. *Jnana* (T. *yeshe*, wisdom) is the wisdom-activity of enlightenment, transcending all dualistic conception. One's being is spontaneously wise, without needing to seek for it. The Tibetan term means "primordially knowing."

7. *The Mandala of Unconditioned Being*

1. Amrita is blessed liquor, used in vajrayana meditation practices.

2. The yanas ("vehicles") in Buddhism are progressive levels of intellectual teachings and meditative practices. The three main yanas are hinayana ("small vehicle"), mahayana ("great vehicle"), and vajrayana ("indestructible vehicle"). The vajrayana is composed of six subsidiary yanas, making nine in all.

3. Mahakalas are wrathful deities whose function is to protect the practitioner from deceptions and sidetracks.

PART TWO

1. The Basic Ground

1. This refers to the Buddhist teaching of the eight consciousnesses, which originated in the Yogachara school. The first five are the five sense consciousnesses. The sixth is mind (S. *mano-vijnana*, T. *yi kyi nampar shepa*), which coordinates the data of the sense consciousnesses (so that, e.g., the color, shape, and odor of a lemon are ascribed to the same object). The seventh consciousness (S. *klishta-manas*, T. *nyön yi*) is the cloudy mind that instigates subjectivity, or self-consciousness. It carries the embryonic sense of duality. The eighth consciousness (S. *alaya-vijnana*, T. *künshi nam-*

par shepa) is the relatively undifferentiated basic, or "storehouse," consciousness. It is called the storehouse consciousness because it carries the karmic tendencies that originate from past karma and generate new karma when elaborated by the other seven consciousnesses. The new activity in turn leaves fresh karmic traces in the alaya, so that an endless cycle is perpetuated.

2. The Birth of the Path

1. See preceding note.

2. See following note.

5. A Glimpse of the Five Buddha Families

1. In the discussion that follows the Vidyadhara makes the traditional vajrayana correlation between the five buddha families and the five skandhas, the five functional building blocks of ego. The five buddha families are given in the order buddha, ratna, padma, karma, and vajra and correlated respectively with the skandhas of form (S. *rupa*, T. *suk*), feeling (S. *vedana*, T. *tsorwa*), impulse (S. *samjna*, T. *dushe*), concept (S. *samskara*, T. *dujé*), and consciousness (S. *vijnana*, T. *nampar shepa*). The Vidyadhara would later adopt the translation "perception" rather than "impulse" for the third skandha, and "formation" rather than "concept" for the fourth skandha.

2. The questioner is alluding to the Vidyadhara's description of the development of ego in *Cutting Through Spiritual Materialism* (Boston & London: Shambhala Publications, 1987). The birth of duality in the first skandha is described in terms of an open expanse of desert in which one grain of sand sticks out its neck and catches a glimpse of itself (p. 125).

Appendix
Transliterations of Tibetan Terms

duje	*'du byed*
dushe	*'du shes*
gashi	*rgashi*
jinpa	*sbyinpa*
khenpo	*mkhan po*
kün shi	*kun gzhi*
künshi nampar shepa	*kun gzhi rnam par shes pa*
kyeche druk	*skye mched drug*
kyewa	*skye ba*
kyilkhor	*dkyil 'khor*
kyorpön	*skyor dpon*
la da wa	*la bzla ba*
ma rikpa	*ma rig pa*
ming dang suk	*ming dang gzugs*
nampar	*rnam par*
nyewar lenpa	*nye bar len pa*
nyi-me	*gnyis med*
nyön yi	*nyon yid*
rekpa	*reg pa*

sampten	*bsam gtan*
sang thal	*zang thal*
sepa	*sred pa*
sherab	*shes rab*
sipa	*srid pa*
sopa	*bzod pa*
suk	*gzugs*
tsondru	*btson 'gru*
tsorwa	*tshorba*
tsultrim	*tshul khrims*
tülku	*sprulsku*
yi	*yid*

About the Author

Ven. Chögyam Trungpa was born in the province of Kham in Eastern Tibet in 1940. When he was just thirteen months old, Chögyam Trungpa was recognized as a major *tülku,* or incarnate teacher. According to Tibetan tradition, an enlightened teacher is capable, based on his or her vow of compassion, of reincarnating in human form over a succession of generations. Before dying, such a teacher leaves a letter or other clues as to the whereabouts of the next incarnation. Later, students and other realized teachers look through these clues and, based on careful examination of dreams and visions, conduct searches to discover and recognize the successor. Thus, particular lines of teaching are formed, in some cases extending over several centuries. Chögyam Trungpa was the eleventh in the teaching lineage known as the Trungpa tülkus.

Once young tülkus are recognized, they enter a period of intensive training in the theory and practice of the Buddhist teachings. Trungpa Rinpoche (*Rinpoche* being an honorific title meaning "precious one"), after being enthroned as supreme abbot of Surmang Monasteries and governor of Surmang District, began a period of training that would last eighteen years, until his departure from Tibet in 1959. As a Kagyü tülku, his training was based on the systematic practice of meditation and on refined theoretical understanding of Buddhist philosophy. One of the four great lineages of Tibet, the Kagyü is known as the "practice lineage."

At the age of eight, Trungpa Rinpoche received ordination as a novice monk. After his ordination, he engaged in intensive study and practice of the traditional monastic disciplines as well as in the arts of calligraphy, thangka painting, and monastic dance. His primary teachers were Jamgön Kongtrül of Sechen and Khenpo Kangshar—leading teachers in the Nyingma and Kagyü lineages. In 1958, at the age of eighteen, Trungpa Rinpoche completed his studies, receiving the degree of *kyorpön* (doctor of divinity) and *khenpo* (master of studies). He also received full monastic ordination.

The late fifties were a time of great upheaval in Tibet. As it became clear that the Chinese Communists intended to take over the country by force, many people, both monastic and lay, fled the country. Trungpa Rinpoche spent many harrowing months trekking over the Himalayas (described in his book *Born in Tibet*). After narrowly escaping capture by the Chinese, he at last reached India in 1959. While in India, Trungpa Rinpoche was appointed by His Holiness Tenzin Gyatso, the fourteenth Dalai Lama, to serve as spiritual advisor to the Young Lamas Home School in Dalhousie, India. He served in this capacity from 1959 to 1963.

Trungpa Rinpoche's first opportunity to encounter the West came when he received a Spaulding sponsorship to attend Oxford University. At Oxford he studied comparative religion, philosophy, and fine arts. He also studied Japanese flower arranging, receiving a degree from the Sogetsu School. While in England, Trungpa Rinpoche began to instruct Western students in the *dharma* (the teachings of the Buddha), and in 1968 he founded the Samye Ling Meditation Centre in Dumfriesshire, Scotland. During this period he also published his first two books, both in English: *Born in Tibet* and *Meditation in Action.*

In 1969, Trungpa Rinpoche traveled to Bhutan, where he entered into a solitary meditation retreat. This retreat marked a pivotal change in his approach to teaching. Immediately upon returning he became a lay person, putting aside his monastic robes and dressing in ordinary Western attire. He also married a young Englishwoman, and together they left Scotland and moved to North America. Many of his early students found these changes shocking and upsetting. However, he expressed a conviction that, in order to take root in the West, the dharma needed to be taught free from cultural trappings and religious fascination.

During the seventies America was in a period of political and cultural ferment. It was a time of fascination with the East. Trungpa Rinpoche criticized the materialistic and commercialized approach to spirituality he encountered, describing it as a "spiritual supermarket." In his lectures, and in his books *Cutting Through Spiritual Materialism* and *The Myth of Freedom,* he pointed to the simplicity and directness of the practice of sitting meditation as the way to cut through such distortions of the spiritual journey.

During his seventeen years of teaching in North America, Trungpa Rinpoche developed a reputation as a dynamic and controversial teacher. Due to his proficiency in the English language, he was one of the first lamas who could speak to Western students directly, without the aid of a translator. Traveling extensively throughout North America and Europe, Trungpa Rinpoche gave hundreds of talks and seminars. He established major centers in Vermont, Colorado, and Nova Scotia, as well as many smaller meditation and study centers in cities throughout North America and Europe. Vajradhatu was formed in 1973 as the central administrative body of this network.

In 1974, Trungpa Rinpoche founded the Naropa Institute, which became the only accredited Buddhist-inspired university in North America. He lectured extensively at the Institute, and his book *Journey Without Goal* is based on a course he taught there. In 1976, he established the Shambhala Training program, a series of weekend programs and seminars that provides instruction in meditation practice within a secular setting. His book *Shambhala: The Sacred Path of the Warrior* gives an overview of the Shambhala teachings.

Trungpa Rinpoche was also active in the field of translation. Working with Francesca Fremantle, he rendered a new translation of *The Tibetan Book of the Dead,* which was published in 1975. Later he formed the Nalanda Translation Committee, in order to translate texts and liturgies for his own students as well as to make important texts available publicly.

Trungpa Rinpoche was also known for his interest in the arts, and particularly for his insights into the relationship between contemplative discipline and the artistic process. His own art work included calligraphy, painting, flower arranging, poetry, playwriting, and environmental installations. In addition, at the Naropa Institute, he created an educational atmosphere that attracted many leading artists and poets. The exploration of the creative process in light of contemplative training continues there as a provocative dialogue. Trungpa Rinpoche also published two books of poetry: *Mudra* and *First Thought Best Thought.*

Trungpa Rinpoche's published books represent only a fraction of the rich legacy of his teachings. During his seventeen years of teaching in North America, he crafted the structures necessary to provide his students with thorough, systematic training in the dharma. From introductory talks and courses to advanced group retreat practices, these programs emphasize a balance of study and practice, of intellect and intuition. Students at all levels can pursue their interest in meditation and the Buddhist path through these many forms of training. Senior students of Trungpa Rinpoche continue to be involved in both teaching and meditation instruction in such programs. In addition to his extensive teachings in the Buddhist tradition, Trungpa Rinpoche also placed great emphasis on the Shambhala teachings, which stress the importance of mind-training, as distinct from religious practice; community involvement and the creation of an enlightened society; and appreciation of one's day-to-day life.

Trungpa Rinpoche·passed away in 1987, at the age of forty-seven. He is survived by his wife Diana and five sons. By the time of his death, Trungpa Rinpoche had become known as a pivotal figure in introducing dharma to the Western world. The joining of his great appreciation for Western culture and his deep understanding of his own tradition led to a revolutionary approach to teaching the dharma, in which the most ancient and profound teachings were presented in a thoroughly contemporary way. Trungpa Rinpoche was known for his fearless proclamation of the dharma: free from hesitation, true to the purity of the tradition, and utterly fresh. May these teachings take root and flourish for the benefit of all sentient beings.

Meditation Center Information

For further information regarding meditation or inquiries about a dharma center near you, please contact one of the following centers:

Karme-Chöling
Star Route
Barnet, VT 05821
(802) 633-2384

Rocky Mountain Dharma Center
4921 County Road 68C
Red Feather Lakes, CO 80545
(303) 881-2184

Vajradhatu Europe
Zwetchenweg 23
D3550 Marburg
Germany
49 6421 46363

Vajradhatu International
1084 Tower Road
Halifax, N.S. B3H 2Y5
Canada
(902) 425-4275

Many talks and seminars are available in cassette tape format. For information, call or write:

Vajradhatu Recordings
1084 Tower Road
Halifax, N.S. B3H 2Y5
(902) 421-1550

Index

THE DHARMA OCEAN SERIES